Cambridge Regional Geogr

Editors Harry Tolley, *School of Education*
Keith Orrell, *Department of Educa*

Northern Ireland

Godfrey Dalton
Former Senior Lecturer in Education
Queens University, Belfast

and

Peter Murray
Former Head of Geography Department
Grosvenor High School, Belfast

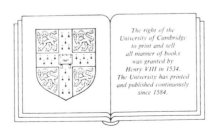

Cambridge University Press

Cambridge
New York   New Rochelle   Melbourne   Sydney

Published by the Press Syndicate of the University of Cambridge
The Pitt Building, Trumpington Street, Cambridge CB2 1RP
32 East 57th Street, New York, NY 10022, USA
10 Stamford Road, Oakleigh Melbourne 3166, Australia

© Cambridge University Press 1987

First published 1987

Printed in Great Britain by
The University Press, Cambridge

British Library Cataloguing in Publication Data
Dalton, Godfrey
Northern Ireland.—(Cambridge regional geography)
1. Anthropo-geography—Northern Ireland
I. Title II. Murray, Peter
304.2'09416 GF561

ISBN 0 521 27454 0

Acknowledgements

The Publishers would like to thank the following for permission to reproduce illustrations: The British Library (fig. 5.4); City of Belfast Official Industrial Handbook (fig. 7.4); E. Connelly (fig. 8.11); Craigavon Borough Council (fig. 6.20); F. C. Curragh (figs. 3.9, 4.17); Harland and Wolff Ltd (figs. 7.9(a) and (b), 7.10); International Linen Promotion, London (fig. 7.5); Larne Harbour Ltd (fig. 8.10); Loughall Horticultural Centre (W. H. Dawson) (fig. 4.6); N. C. Mitchel (figs. 3.1, 4.12(a) and (b), 4.13, 4.14(b), 5.3, 7.6); Northern Ireland Tourist Board (figs. 1.7, 3.3, 3.6, 8.4); Ordnance Survey of Northern Ireland, reproduced with the sanction of the Controller of HM Stationery Office, Crown Copyright reserved (fig. 1.4); Short Bros. (fig. 8.12); J. Woods (fig. 6.3).

The publishers also thank the 1981 Census of Northern Ireland for supplying population figures, the Meteorological Office for climate statistics and the Department of Agriculture for agricultural statistics, used throughout this book; and A. Robinson and F. Boal for statistics on p. 9 and pp. 61–3 respectively.

Cover design by Pavel Büchler.

WV

Contents

1 The borders of Northern Ireland   5

2 The people   11

3 The land   21

4 People on the land   30

5 Human landscapes   44

6 Patterns in the city   54

7 Establishing industries   67

8 Exchanging goods and services   81

9 Northern Ireland in context   90

   Index   95

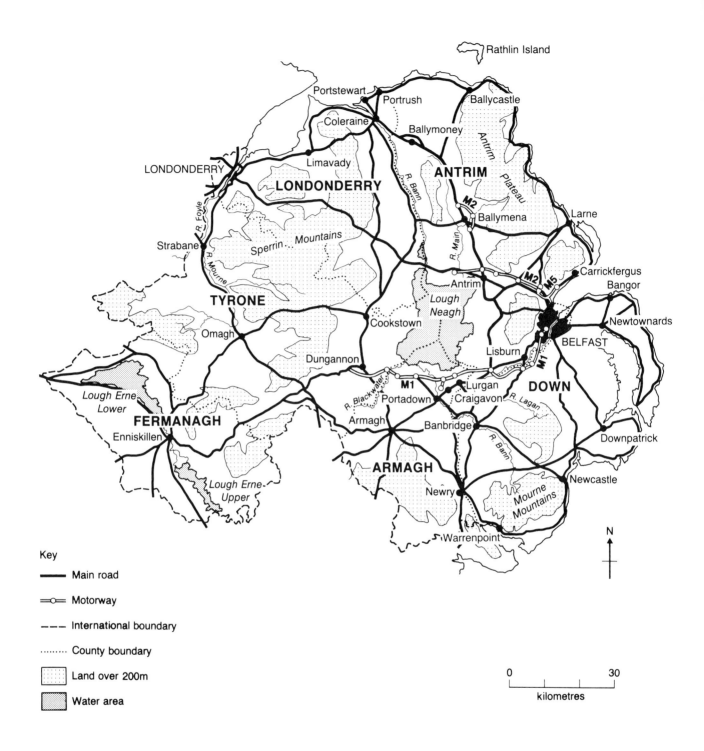

Fig. 1.1. Northern Ireland.

1 The borders of Northern Ireland

The **British Isles** includes the two sovereign states of the Republic of Ireland and the United Kingdom.
The **United Kingdom** includes Great Britain (the mainland) and Northern Ireland.
(The word 'British' is not a precise term, e.g. British Army, British Airways should strictly be UK Army, UK Airways.)
Great Britain includes England, Scotland and Wales (but *not* Northern Ireland).

If you were a world dictator faced with the task of dividing up the world into regions, what would you use as boundaries for the regions – mountain ranges, rivers, deserts?

It may surprise you to find that obvious physical features often do not coincide with the boundaries of states. Consider the wide stretch of water called the Irish Sea. It seems at first glance to be a perfect dividing feature between **Great Britain** and Ireland. The English Channel equally obviously separates the **British Isles** from Continental countries. Yet these seas have often been ignored. The map of the kingdom of Dalriada (fig. 1.2) is one example. In medieval times, the king of England was often ruling parts of what is today the country of France. For several periods in more recent times representatives of the people of Ireland have travelled across the Irish Sea to sit in the parliament in England.

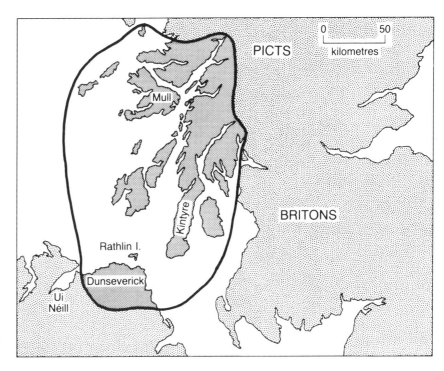

Fig. 1.2. The kingdom of Dalriada about AD 500.

Rivers are no better as natural boundaries. The famous River Rhine was never a satisfactory frontier between France and Germany. We do use the River Foyle for a small part of the western boundary of Northern Ireland: the towns of Strabane (Northern Ireland) and Lifford (Republic of Ireland) are separated only by the river. Further north the river would make an odd boundary, for it flows through the middle of a city (fig. 1.3).

Further on where the river widens into an estuary, more problems arise. When a boat called the *Sally-En* was sunk near Moville, there was

5

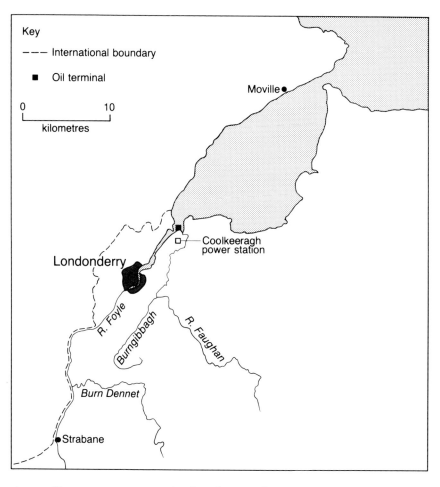

Fig. 1.3. The River Foyle estuary.

strong disagreement as to whether the wreck was in the **United Kingdom** or in the Republic. Which government should pay the cost of salvaging it? Should the border be at an equal distance from each shore or should it be drawn down the centre of the navigable channel which at this point hugs the Donegal shore? Oddly enough the pilots for guiding boats entering and leaving the United Kingdom port are based on the Irish side at Moville.

Carlingford Lough, the southern border of Northern Ireland, presents fewer such problems but even there a glance at a map makes it clear that the river would not be a good natural boundary further inland. Nor is a river satisfactory as a border at Pettigoe (fig. 1.4).

Even more surprising, mountainous areas do not always form good borders. In Northern Ireland the most prominently hilly areas, the Mourne Mountains and the Sperrins, are wholly within the province. The only high point on the boundary is one of the peaks in the range of the Leitrim Hills.

It seems that the most successful borders between states in the world as a whole are drawn across areas of thinly populated land. Small parts around the Northern Ireland boundary could be so described but most of the border area is characterised by rolling hills and scattered farmsteads. Yet the border is there. In peaceful times it is often ignored, as in the early 1960s. In stressful times, it is a very real part of the environment. Why then was the boundary drawn where it is?

The land border of Northern Ireland can only be explained if we

Fig. 1.4. Air photograph of Pettigoe. The River Termon marks the international boundary – it cuts the village into two parts.

consider how the 'feelings' of people have grown over centuries. Many events, personalities and memories affect the way people develop a sense of nationhood. The history of the inhabitants of the ancient province of Ulster was rather different from that of the rest of the island. When most parts of Ireland were separating from the United Kingdom in 1920 the feelings of the majority of the people of the north were strongly expressed against the idea of an independent Ireland. They wanted to remain under the government of Westminster (fig. 1.5). So in 1921 Ireland was divided, at least for a time, with the agreement of both the Dublin and Westminster authorities.

Decisions about where to draw the border had to be made on the basis of majority feeling. There was no time for detailed planning. It seemed simplest to use the county boundaries originally devised before the seventeenth century. Donegal, Cavan and Monaghan were excluded from Northern Ireland because the majority in those counties did not favour the union with Great Britain; the rest of Ulster was included in the northern state. 'Feelings' were more dominant than any physical features.

A border commission in 1926 recommended a few minor changes (fig. 1.6) but by that time it was not considered wise to tamper with the original hurried decision. This was because once a boundary is drawn, differences between the two sides develop over the years through

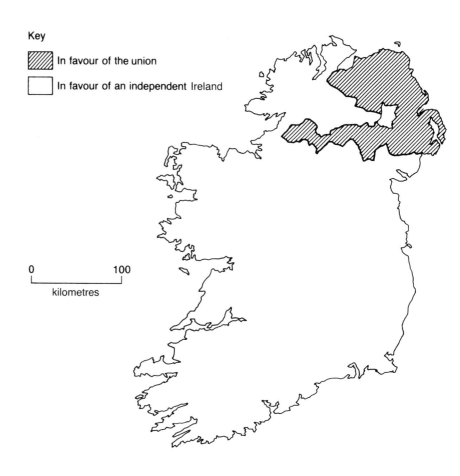

Fig. 1.5. Result of the 1918 General Election in Ireland. Sinn Féin won 73 seats, the Unionists 26 seats and the Parliamentary Party 6 seats.

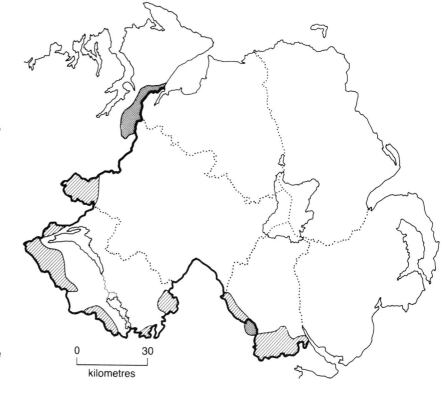

Fig. 1.6. Proposals for changes of the border made by the Irish Commission, 1925.

The **European Economic Community** (EEC), which was founded in 1958, has grown from six member countries to twelve. Its members are pledged to work together economically for the benefit of all; some think of the Community as the first stage towards a new political unity, the United States of Europe.

different electoral systems and political policies, different agricultural and industrial subsidies, educational and welfare provisions, different tax systems, emblems and uniforms, laws and traditions. In many obvious and intangible ways the two parts have grown more and more different.

A boundary that depends on 'feelings' is not however permanent, for 'feelings' do change. We don't know in what way they will change in the future. It could be imagined that one day there might be a state including the whole of these Atlantic islands. We may become 'Atlantans' with the Scots, Welsh and English! Then the Irish Sea would become again an 'inland sea', not a boundary at all.

The **European Economic Community** (EEC) is also causing economic changes.

Can you name the EEC's twelve member countries?

Economies change much more quickly than 'feelings'. For example, nearly half of Warrenpoint's exports, after it had been modernised in the 1970s, came from the Republic and over 60% of its grain imports crossed the border to the south. Again, much road traffic from the Republic to the mainland and the Continent travels through the North to a 'Larne to Great Britain' ferry. Several EEC grants for development are for areas which straddle the border (and see fig. 1.7). Will a border which is ignored economically survive? We don't know.

Perhaps we may one day begin to feel ourselves to be 'Europeans' just in the same way as the people of California think of themselves as Americans. We should then have the problem of defining new boundaries between the EEC and 'the others'.

Would you like to tackle that task? Where, do you feel, is the proper boundary for the European Community? Does it follow any physical features? Would you feel proud to belong to the 'European' nation?

Exercises

1. In 1969, 533 primary schoolchildren in Londonderry were asked: 'What is the capital of the country in which Derry is situated?'
Here are the results (in %).

Dublin	Belfast	London	Other	Don't know
29.0	47.7	1.6	10.2	11.5

How would you explain these results? Could you express your ideas in the form of a hypothesis? How would you set about testing your hypothesis to see if it is true? (Think about how the replies might differ from different kinds of schools.)

Fig. 1.7. Tourist literature straddles the border, as this photograph of a tourist map cover shows.

2. Can you list the differences that have developed between the Republic and Northern Ireland since the drawing of the border? Which of the institutions listed below indicate (a) the distinctiveness of Northern Ireland (b) connections with Great Britain (c) connections with the Republic of Ireland (d) a combination of (b) and (c)?

Royal Ulster Constabulary	Currency
Irish rugby team	Church of Ireland
School system	Elections
National Health Insurance	Road signs
Youth Hostel Association	Membership of the EEC

3. There are many artificial boundaries in the world. What marks the border between
   (a) Canada and the USA?
   (b) Turkey and Greece?
   (c) Zambia and Angola?
   (d) Iraq and Saudi Arabia?
   (e) India and Pakistan?

   Can you find in your atlas examples where natural features do seem to make firm political boundaries? (Consider France and Spain – but don't forget the Basque people.)

4. Compare the islands listed in the margin with the island of Ireland (area 84,400 km^2). Which are (a) states (b) divided into different states (c) partly or wholly governed from a mainland?

	Area (km^2)
Borneo	751,000
Cyprus	9,251
Hawaii	16,400
Hispaniola	76,192
Newfoundland	112,299
Sardinia	23,812
Sicily	25,710
Sri Lanka	65,610
Tasmania	68,332
Tierra del Fuego	73,746

2 The people

Most of our knowledge about the people of Northern Ireland is obtained from the ten-yearly census. Every household is given a census form (fig. 2.1) and details of everyone in the house on census night are recorded. The information on hundreds of thousands of forms has then to be transferred to a computer record before we can use it to understand the geography of Northern Ireland. The analysis is also important to many government departments. They have to plan education, organise

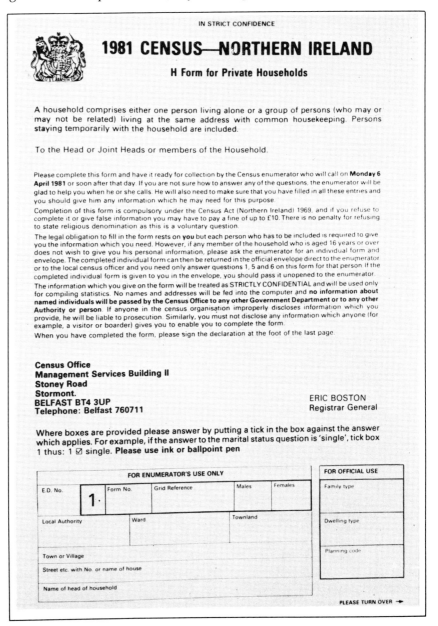

Fig. 2.1. A form for the 1981 census – Northern Ireland.

hospitals and prepare transport plans. Businessmen arranging to make and sell goods need to advertise and to recruit labour, and they need to know where people live. Some countries are seriously handicapped by inaccurate census figures caused by some people's fear of being counted: there were some problems of people refusing to record themselves even in Northern Ireland in 1981.

You would think that the simplest map to draw from the census material would be one to show where people are living. The details in columns 1 and 2 of Table 1 are from the 1981 census. We shall have to assume that the first column is right, although officially it is estimated that about 19,000 people were not recorded (and that figure is probably underestimated).

Table 1 *Population census, 1981.*

District	1 Numbers of people counted	2 Area km²	3 Population density per km²
Antrim	44,384	563	79
Ards	57,626	369	156
Armagh	47,618	672	71
Ballymena	54,426	638	85
Ballymoney	22,873	419	55
Banbridge	29,885	444	67
Belfast	295,223	140	2,108
Carrickfergus	28,458	87	327
Castlereagh	60,757	85	715
Coleraine	46,272	482	96
Cookstown	26,624	623	43
Craigavon	71,202	382	186
Down	52,869	646	82
Dungannon	41,073	779	53
Fermanagh	51,008	1,875	27
Larne	28,929	338	86
Limavady	26,270	587	45
Lisburn	82,091	444	185
Londonderry	83,384	375	222
Magherafelt	30,825	563	55
Moyle	14,252	495	29
Newry & Mourne	72,243	893	81
Newtownabbey	71,631	152	471
North Down	65,849	73	902
Omagh	41,159	1,129	36
Strabane	35,028	867	40
Northern Ireland	1,481,959	14,120	

The population density (column 3) can easily be calculated, but again we are making assumptions. For example, 176 km² of Fermanagh District is part of Lough Erne itself. Antrim, Craigavon and Cookstown districts are similarly affected.

Can you think why? (Almost every district includes some sea or inland water area.)

There are also many uninhabited land areas. Fig. 2.2 is only a

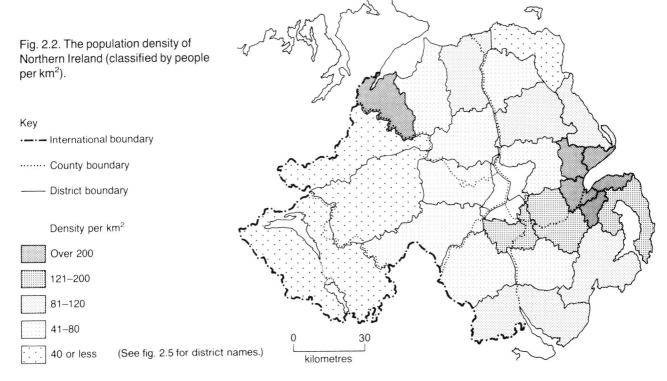

Fig. 2.2. The population density of Northern Ireland (classified by people per km²).

Key
- ⋅—⋅— International boundary
- ⋯⋯⋯ County boundary
- ——— District boundary

Density per km²
- Over 200
- 121–200
- 81–120
- 41–80
- 40 or less

(See fig. 2.5 for district names.)

generalised picture. Moyle District has an average of 29 people per km². No one however lives on Fairhead or high on Knocklayd. Few live around the Causeway, yet there are over 1,000 people living in the square kilometre which includes Bushmills. Such examples occur all over the province. Obviously this simple density map hides many irregularities in the distribution of people. Is there not a better way of putting our census count on a map?

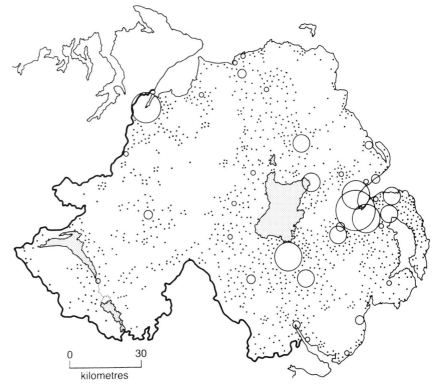

Fig. 2.3. The population density of Northern Ireland (a dot distribution map). The circle for Belfast is still too small, since it represents 295,000 people. What towns do the other large circles represent?

Key — Towns with population of
- More than 100,000
- 50–100,000
- 20–50,000
- 10–20,000
- 5–10,000

· 500 people

13

We can try using one dot to represent a number of people, say 500. We could then place the dots where people actually live and leave the uninhabited part of each district blank (fig. 2.3). We call this a dot distribution map.

Can you see what problems have arisen with this method? How many dots would be needed to mark Belfast?

Mapmakers use different-sized circles to represent different sizes of towns. Some mapmakers resort to drawing spheres to give a better pictorial impression of the concentration of people in the small area of large towns.

Whatever method we use it is clear that there is a very heavy concentration of people living around Belfast. If we include the built-up area of Newtownabbey and Carrickfergus to the north, Lisburn in the south-west, Castlereagh in the south-east and the North Down coast, we include 41% of Northern Ireland's population. Indeed we have only to add the adjacent towns of Antrim, Larne, Bangor, Newtownards and Craigavon and we have more than 54% of the population on about one-sixth of the total area of the province.

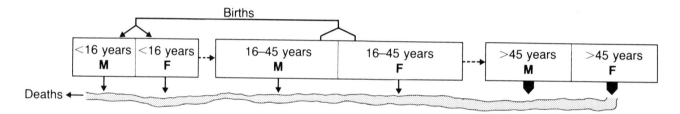

Fig. 2.4. A model of natural changes.

Gains and losses

The last census was taken on 5 April 1981. It is a snapshot of where everyone was at midnight on that day. The picture should be a moving picture, of course, for population is always changing.

Fig. 2.4 refers to natural changes, the differences resulting from births and deaths. The rate of natural change is affected by social factors.

Which of the following changes would increase and which would decrease the speed of population increase or decrease?
(a) Wider acceptance of contraceptives and abortion.
(b) Better medical provision for old people.
(c) Increase in the amount of child benefit.
(d) A change in fashion leading to marriage at an earlier date (this would have a very significant long-term effect if the children followed the parents' example).
(e) A world war.

Another very important factor in population change in Northern Ireland is migration. The decision to move to a different part of the province or out of it is usually based on what are believed to be the advantages of the new area compared with the disadvantages of the home area. Fig. 2.5 shows the natural increase/decrease in each of the areas of Northern Ireland between 1971 and 1981. The abnormal increase in Antrim is probably due to the recent movement into southern Antrim of many young couples. Migration of many people from the western areas is not a new pattern. For many decades people have left the apparent difficulties of living in the west to try to better themselves in the bigger towns of the east.

counterurbanisation
Movement of population away from large cities to semi-rural areas or small 'commuter' towns.

However, notice what the map shows about Belfast. Not only is natural increase very small; the loss by migration is enormous. This reflects the greater use of personal and public transport these days and the setting up of industries in the peripheral areas of North Down and south Antrim which 'pulls' people towards them. The problems of city life have had a 'push' effect on people who were hesitating about moving out. The word **counterurbanisation** has been invented to describe this tendency.

Push and pull effects have varied through history. In the seventeenth century the planters migrated from the mainland into the rural areas of Ulster, pulled by the land which was available for them. Later the attractions of the New World pulled migrants from the poorer agricultural areas in Ireland. The famine in the 1840s obviously had a push effect. In the late nineteenth century the attraction was to the urban area of Belfast or to Great Britain where paid work was available. The larger towns pulled the hardest. Nowadays with easier commuting facilities and more congestion in city centres, people have tended to be pulled to pleasanter suburbs and small towns, being pushed by the rigours of city life.

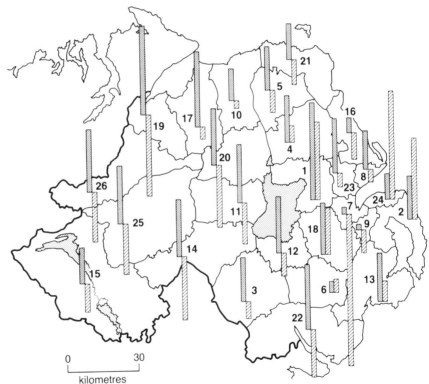

Fig. 2.5. Northern Ireland intercensal change, 1971–81. In general terms, where did the largest natural increases take place?

Key

Natural increase 1971–81 (excess births over deaths)

Migration 1971–81

1 cm = 7%

Upward bars show increases
Downward bars show decreases

1	Antrim	14	Dungannon
2	Ards	15	Fermanagh
3	Armagh	16	Larne
4	Ballymena	17	Limavady
5	Ballymoney	18	Lisburn
6	Banbridge	19	Londonderry
7	Belfast	20	Magherafelt
8	Carrickfergus	21	Moyle
9	Castlereagh	22	Newry & Mourne
10	Coleraine	23	Newtownabbey
11	Cookstown	24	North Down
12	Craigavon	25	Omagh
13	Down	26	Strabane

Forecasting: chancy but necessary

Take a look at fig. 2.6(a). It could have been drawn after the 1971 census. Another way of census mapping helps in making predictions. We can draw age-sex pyramids. If we had considered the age-sex pyramid for 1971 (fig. 2.7) we should have noticed the bulge of children in the 4- to 8-year age groups and the lower number of infants.

Forecasts of the percentage of population which will be economically

Fig. 2.6. Population trends in Northern Ireland:
(a) 1821–1971. Which way would you have expected the graph line to move by 1981: A, B or C? The correct answer can be seen by examining (b).
(b) 1951–81. It's even more hazardous to make predictions for 1991.

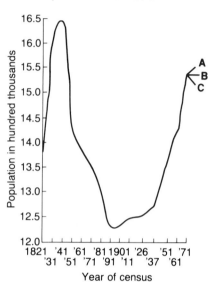

(a)

active are obviously important, because they relate to taxation, health insurance, transport systems and many other features of modern life. Only people between the ages of 16 and 64 are regarded as economically productive. Those people must produce both for themselves *and* for children and retired people.

Although fig. 2.5 shows the migration within Northern Ireland between 1971 and 1981, it doesn't show the social consequences. Often, an ageing and declining workforce is left behind, with little to look forward to but a further reduction of economic activity. In the receiving areas, the relatively young immigrants tend to swamp the social services, maternity clinics and schools (there are no problems of classes being too small), and there may well be severe competition for housing. Age-sex pyramids show such characteristics (fig. 2.8).

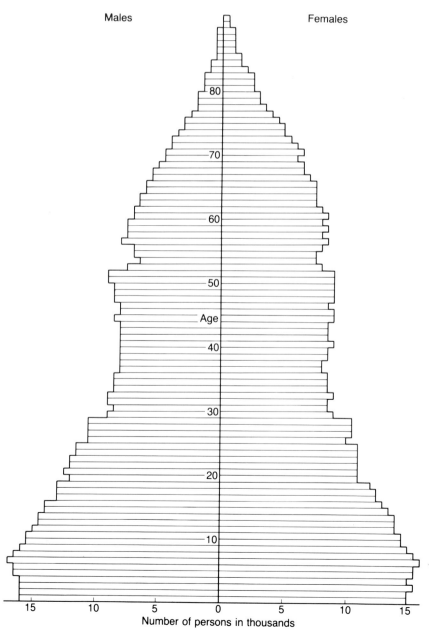

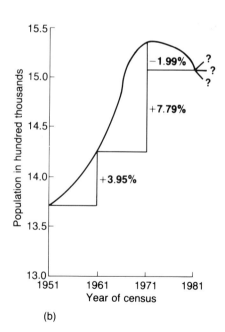

(b)

Fig. 2.7. The age-sex pyramid for Northern Ireland, 1971.

Social information

The census count not only tells us where we all live and how population distribution is changing. It also tells us how we heat our homes, how many cars we use, what religion we profess, what advanced education we have had, and so on. Many of these facts can be shown diagrammatically or mapped to show distributions. Here are three examples.

1. Fig. 2.9 shows the distribution of houses in Northern Ireland with cavity wall insulation. How can we explain it? You could make some suggestions or hypotheses and then discuss how they could be proved or disproved. Here are three hypotheses (you may be able to suggest some more).
   (a) Householders in the more central parts of the province experience slightly greater extremes of temperature than on the east coast. They therefore take a greater interest in insulating their homes.
   (b) The idea of cavity wall insulation is rather new. New ideas tend to start in the capital and slowly diffuse out to the periphery. Insulation ideas have not yet fully reached the farthest parts of the province.
   (c) Detached houses, having more exterior walls, lose heat rather quickly. Insulation is therefore considered more necessary amongst more wealthy owner-occupiers than amongst terrace-house dwellers.

Fig. 2.8. (a) the age-sex pyramid for Conlig, County Down, 1981.
(b) The age-sex pyramid for Suffolk, 1981. Suffolk is a suburb of Belfast. Few people will be retiring here during the next fifteen years compared with the number of school leavers. The young people are likely to be unemployed unless emigration takes place or new employment possibilities are introduced within commuting distance.

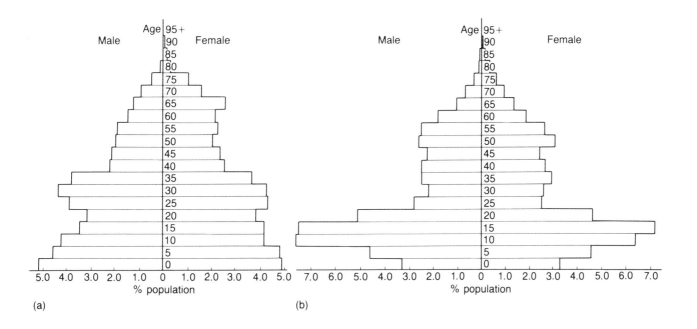

2. The question about religion on the census form was a voluntary one and over 275,000 (18% of those counted) declined to answer; 4,563 declared that they were not Christian, but Muslims, Jews, atheists, etc. (fig. 2.10). With the aid of a computer, it is easy to analyse the statistics and answer particular questions. You may like to make guesses at the answers to some of the following questions (you will find the correct answers on p. 94).
   (a) In which local government areas are Roman Catholics in a majority?
   (b) In which local government areas do Methodists form a sizeable percentage of the population?
   (c) Is there any difference between males and females in church allegiance?

Fig. 2.9. Percentage of houses with cavity wall insulation.

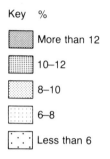

Key %
- More than 12
- 10–12
- 8–10
- 6–8
- Less than 6

3. There are no questions on the census directly about wealth or income. If we want to draw a map to show how affluence is distributed, we shall have to use what are called 'indicators'. Which of the following do you think indicates wealth best?
   (a) Absence of overcrowding in homes, that is, at least one room (excluding small kitchen, toilet, etc.) per person in the household.
   (b) Possession of three or more cars per household.
   (c) Central heating in houses.
   (d) A high percentage of economically active persons actually working (i.e. few adults without paid work).

Fig. 2.10. Religious denominations in Northern Ireland.

The future

The population picture is always changing. Some future problems we can already foresee are:
(a) overpopulation in some areas;
(b) unequal distribution of wealth;
(c) the need for home-grown development especially in less prosperous areas;
(d) the provision for the growing percentage of retired people.

Some past solutions such as emigration are unlikely options for the future. Geographers will be watching to see what other solutions people find.

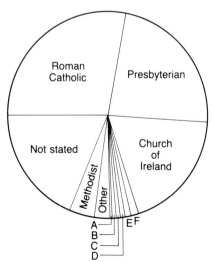

A Non-Christian
B Indefinite answer
C Free Presbyterian
D Brethren
E Protestant
F Baptist

Exercises

1. In Table 2 the percentage of households with characteristics of affluence has been calculated for each district, and then ranked (Belfast has been omitted because of its dominance).

Table 2 *The distribution of possible indicators of affluence in Northern Ireland.*

District	Free from overcrowding (i)	Possessing 3 or more cars (ii)	Houses centrally heated (iii)	Economically active people in jobs (iv)
Antrim	10	15	2	8
Ards	5	6	10	3
Armagh	13	1	14	12
Ballymena	8	12	8	6
Ballymoney	15	5	22	15
Banbridge	12	2	16	7
Carrickfergus	3	24	13	11
Castlereagh	2	14	3	2
Coleraine	9	18	9	14
Cookstown	17	3	17	22
Craigavon	11	16	6	13
Down	14	9	11	9
Dungannon	18	4	23	18
Fermanagh	16	7	18	16
Larne	7	21	19	10
Limavady	23	20	12	20
Lisburn	6	10	5	4
Londonderry	24	25	7	22
Magherafelt	22	8	24	19
Moyle	19	22	25	21
Newry & Mourne	20	17	21	24
Newtownabbey	4	23	4	5
North Down	1	13	1	1
Omagh	21	11	15	17
Strabane	25	19	20	25

The problem is to find which pair of these possibly affluent characteristics correlate best. One of the pairs, (i) and (iv), has been calculated for you (see below) using Spearman's Rank Correlation. A perfect correlation would be 1; a negative correlation would be less than 0 (.6 or more is quite a good correlation). Try to explain the reasons for the answers you get. Does this exercise help you to choose the best indicator of affluence?

Calculation of correlation between (i) and (iv)
(a) Calculate the difference (d) between the rankings for each district: e.g. Antrim is 2, Down is 5.
(b) Square each of these differences (d^2): Antrim is 4, Down is 25.
(c) Add up all these squared differences (Σd^2): the total is 253.
(d) The formula to use to find the correlation R is:

$$R = 1 - \frac{6\Sigma d^2}{n^3 - n}$$

where n is the total number of items, i.e. districts (25).
The calculation therefore is: $1 - 6 \times 253 \div (25^3 - 25)$
$= 1 - 0.097 = .9$ (a very high correlation)

2. Try to explain to an unco-operative householder who is being asked to fill in a census form why a province like Northern Ireland needs to obtain population data and needs to attempt to forecast future population changes.

Table 3 *Population of towns over 10,000 in Northern Ireland.*

	Thousands
Belfast	295
Londonderry	62
Newtownabbey	56
Craigavon	52
Bangor	46
Lisburn	40
Ballymena	28
Antrim	22
Newtownards	20
Newry	19
Larne	18
Carrickfergus	17
Coleraine	15
Dunmurry	14
Omagh	14
Armagh	12
Enniskillen	10
Strabane	10

3. Imagine there is a possibility that your father may have to move from the west of Northern Ireland to where there is a job in the east. What would make you want to (a) stay and (b) move? What obstacles would face you in the move?
4. It has been suggested that the population of a country is like a bath with two taps, a plughole and an overflow. In what ways is this model (a) helpful and (b) weak when applied to Northern Ireland?
5. Table 3 lists eighteen towns with a population of more than 10,000 in rank order. According to a 'rule' devised by looking at many countries, the population of any town in a country can be estimated by the formula:

$$Pi = \frac{K}{Ri}$$

where Pi is the population of the town, K is the population of the largest city in the country, and Ri is the rank of the town.

Belfast is far too dominant for this formula to apply correctly to Northern Ireland. How big should Londonderry be if the formula were correct? How big should your nearest town be? Compare your answers with the actual populations.

3 The land

The beauty of a human figure depends on the skeleton of bones, the condition of the flesh and skin and the style of clothing. A beautiful landscape depends on the solid rocks, the surface deposits, what is growing in the soil and the alterations by man. The bones of the skeleton grow, age and decay; skin wrinkles; flesh contracts; clothing wears out and is patched. How difficult it is to imagine what an old man looked like when he was young! It is also difficult to imagine the beginnings of every hump and valley in the landscape.

When you look at the scenery, remember the processes which have produced the scenery and try to imagine how it came to be as it is – although at this stage you are unlikely to get it right every time.

The rocks: the skeleton of the landscape

Some 500 million years ago, one of the huge slabs or **plates** of the earth's crust drifted into another plate of which the present England and Wales, southern Scotland and southern Ireland were part. The crumbling of the rocks at the line of contact produced mountain chains across what is now our province. They are called the Caledonian Mountains (after Scotland). Most of these have been worn away, but stumps survive in the north and west (fig. 3.1).

Look at fig. 3.2. Imagine a line from Cushendun through Draperstown and Omagh to Castle Archdale. This continues the fault line which forms the very distinctive north-west boundary of the Midland Valley of Scotland. South of this line the rivers from the mountains deposited sediments which became Old Red Sandstone. The parallel fault which continues the line of the southern boundary of the Midland Valley of Scotland runs through the Lagan Valley. To the south of this fault line, ancient rocks are near the surface, and can be seen along the shores of County Down.

Then there were long periods when **sedimentary rocks** were being laid down and later raised above sea level. For example, about 300 million years ago, in the Carboniferous period, thick layers of limestone, sandstone, shale, grit and coal were laid down (fig. 3.3). Most of the later sedimentaries (sandstones, clays and chalk), which were laid down starting in the Triassic age about 200 million years ago, have been worn away or covered by an **igneous rock**.

About 100 million years ago, the plate of which America is a part was tearing itself away from Europe. It left a huge line of weakness in the earth's crust which gave an opportunity for magma to rise. Lava oozed through cracks in the County Antrim area and spread out. This cooled to form the basalt rock of the plateau that stretches today from the Lagan Valley to the north coast, and includes the Giant's Causeway. Westwards, it ends in the scarp face of Binevenagh (350 metres) overlooking the River Roe. Lough Neagh fills a shallow depression in the basalt which is 850 metres thick at this point (fig. 3.4).

---

plate
Large mass of the earth's crust (perhaps as big as a continent or an ocean floor) which, because it is lighter than the semi-molten magma lower down, can drift about (extremely slowly, of course).

sedimentary rocks
Compacted particles of sand, silt, minute sea creatures, coral or fallen trees and plants. Often they build up under water but emerge when the sea level drops. Carboniferous sedimentary rocks can be seen on the coast east of Ballycastle and in the Magho Scarp overlooking Lough Erne and in the Marble Arch area.

igneous rocks
Molten magma which has cooled either on reaching the surface or below other surface rocks.

Fig. 3.1. Slieve Muckish, County Donegal, an example of a harder-than-average Caledonian stump (made of quartzite) in a region of schists of a similar age.

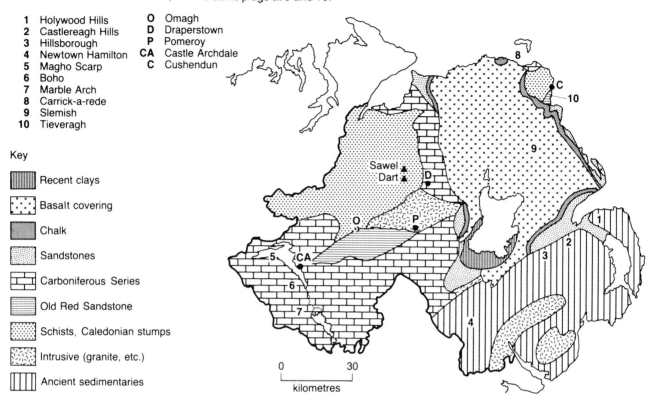

Fig. 3.2. A simplified geological map of Northern Ireland. The remnants of a volcanic crater can be seen at 8, and volcanic plugs at 9 and 10.

1 Holywood Hills
2 Castlereagh Hills
3 Hillsborough
4 Newtown Hamilton
5 Magho Scarp
6 Boho
7 Marble Arch
8 Carrick-a-rede
9 Slemish
10 Tieveragh

O Omagh
D Draperstown
P Pomeroy
CA Castle Archdale
C Cushendun

Key

- Recent clays
- Basalt covering
- Chalk
- Sandstones
- Carboniferous Series
- Old Red Sandstone
- Schists, Caledonian stumps
- Intrusive (granite, etc.)
- Ancient sedimentaries

corrie
A depression in the mountainside with a steep back wall, which was formed by ice. It often contains a small lake.

nunatak
A mountain which stuck out above the ice sheet and so suffered much frost weathering.

erratics
Boulders which are found a long way from where they were formed. Some examples of erratics are pieces of granite from Ailsa Craig (Scotland) found on the north-east shore of Antrim, and rocks from Slieve Gallion found on the northern slopes of the Sperrins.

drumlins
Small hills, each shaped like half an egg cut lengthways. They have a broad end with quite a steep slope and a narrow end with a gentler slope. Like many other words for glacial deposits, it comes from the Irish: *droimnin*.

The Mourne Mountains are made of granite which is basically magma that has cooled slowly deep below the surface and so has had time to crystallise. The area, about 150 km^2, indicates the size of this gigantic 'blister'; we don't of course know its depth. The thick covering of ancient sedimentaries has now been mostly worn away from the mountains, although isolated examples can be found on Slieve Muck and Slievemonaghmore.

Glacial deposits: the skin of the landscape

You wouldn't be able to recognise a friend from his fleshless skeleton. Similarly it is the moulding and particularly the deposition during and after the last Ice Age, which finished about 10,000 years ago, that makes our scenery recognisable and memorable.

Mountain valley glaciation is not spectacular in Northern Ireland. The eastern Mournes do have some fine **corries** in the Pots of Legawherry and Pulgarve on the side of Slieve Commedagh, and frost-shattered peaks such as Slieve Binnian. The Sperrins have neither corries nor **nunataks**. The whole range was over-run and smoothed by northward-moving ice. Elsewhere there are U-shaped valleys.

All kinds of deposition are widespread. **Erratics** prove that ice moved materials around. What else could have moved the granite Cloghmore Rock (fig. 3.5) to its present position on the top of ancient sedimentaries near Rostrevor?

Great swarms of **drumlins** lie across Counties Down, Armagh and

eskers
Long, low, winding ridges of sand and moraine. The word comes from the Irish: *escir* or *sceir*.

terminal moraine
The debris or fragments of rock left at the end of a glacier when it melts. The Kilkeel-Cranfield moraine shows where the Carlingford glacier stopped. The Armoy moraine shows the southern extent of the last Scottish ice advance.

drift
A general term for all glacial deposits including such common material as boulder clay.

Fermanagh and around the Lower Bann (fig. 3.6). Their composition and the direction in which their axes point indicate the route the ice was taking. Other glacial deposits in the form of **eskers**, **terminal moraines** and conical hills of sand and gravel have also affected our scenery and give some clues as to how it developed.

Even more significant is the thick layer of **drift** which covers virtually all the lowland areas. The difference between one field and the next can often partly be explained by different mixes and thicknesses of the drift materials, causing differences in drainage, soil and vegetation.

Deposits also divert rivers. The blocking of the mouth of the River Bann at the time of the approach of Scottish ice resulted in an enlarged Lough Neagh. For a time the lake was so high that the water escaped southwards via the Poyntz Pass to Carlingford Lough, and the pass was made wider and deeper. That was a great help to the canal- and railway-builders of the nineteenth century.

Fig. 3.3 Caves in County Fermanagh, which were formed by underground streams in the very thick Carboniferous limestone rocks, have been opened up for tourists.

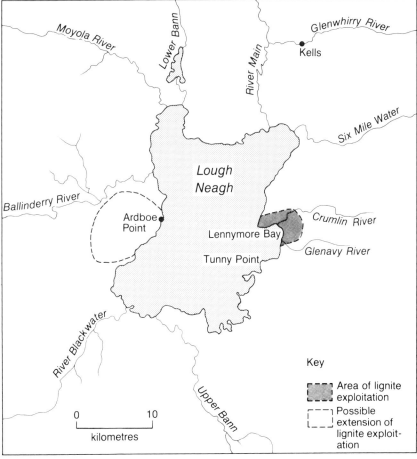

Fig. 3.4. The drainage pattern around Lough Neagh. The catchment area of the Lough is 5,200 km² (43% of the area of Northern Ireland). As pollution of its waters is overcome, the lake is becoming the main source of water for a large proportion of the population.

Fig. 3.5. Cloghmore Rock (a well-known glacial erratic) in Rostrevor Forest Park. What are your feelings when you see graffiti like these in Northern Ireland's beauty spots?

Fig. 3.6. Drumlins partly submerged in Strangford Lough.

Soil and vegetation: the clothing of the landscape

Climate

Soil and vegetation respond to climate – and most of us respond to the weather too, often with a grumble. Even compared with the eastern parts of the British Isles, however, our temperatures are seldom extreme. They vary little between the seasons (from a January mean of about 4°C to a July mean of about 14°C). The diurnal ranges are also usually low. You can see from fig. 3.7 that inland areas are very slightly more 'continental' than coastal areas. The large water areas of Lough Erne and Lough Neagh have moderating effects, of course.

We are more justified in grumbling about the rain. It varies from east to west: the average at Banagher, County Londonderry is 1,270 mm compared with 880 mm at Bangor, County Down, but relief has the greatest effect on its distribution. The rain tends to be of very low intensity (drizzle is characteristic rather than heavy showers) and it thus lasts longer. A consequence is a climate with very low sunshine hours (only about 25% of possible amounts) and heavy cloud (only about 35 days a year are cloudless).

Soils

podzolic soils
They are characterised by the fact that many of the mineral foods and humus have been leached out of the topsoil, and are beyond the reach of small plants.

In a wet climate such as ours, it is sometimes asked whether a well-drained soil is preferable to a waterlogged one? Look at fig. 3.8. Of course it takes many years for these processes to operate, but if they continued we should have widespread **podzolic soils**. Farmers interfere by ploughing the well-drained soils, liming and fertilising with manure so that crops and grass can be grown. Waterlogged soils can also be improved by digging ditches and putting in tunnel drains.

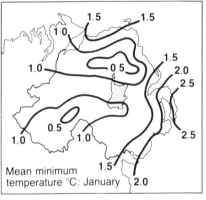

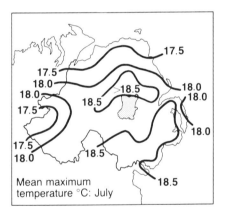

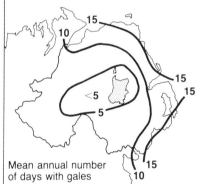

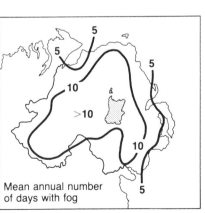

Fig. 3.7. Some climatic details for Northern Ireland.

Vegetation

Ireland's scenery is noted for its greenness, the result of the rain (and fertilisers!). Peat and forest add extra features.

Following the Ice Age, up to 2 metres of peat was laid down over our waterlogged uplands, but much has now been removed by gully erosion, bog bursts, extraction of peat for fuel and possibly by the tramping of many enthusiastic hikers. Peat also developed in old lake beds and in hollows between drumlins (fig. 3.9).

The deciduous woodlands on the hills were cleared by early man (about 1500 BC). The lowland forests were felled by the eighteenth century to clear land for agriculture, and the timber was used for building, fuel and charcoal. Only odd patches remain today, for example in Glenshesk Valley (Ballycastle), Castle Archdale (Fermanagh) and on islands in Lough Neagh. Coniferous Sitka spruce forests now enhance about 5% of the province; more than 80% of these conifers were planted on land which could not be farmed very profitably.

Fig. 3.8. What happens to a well-drained soil in the Northern Ireland climate.

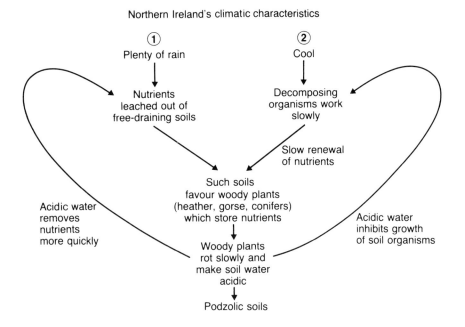

Using the rocks

Physical, economic and social problems have to be tackled when mining of any kind is considered (fig. 3.10).

Problem: Prospecting

Can useful rocks be found in Northern Ireland?
Coal seams, quite near the surface at Ballycastle and at Coalisland, are now exhausted. Bores to locate new seams at Larne, Ballycastle and Magilligan were unsuccessful even though they went more than 1 km deep. Prospecting for oil and gas is in progress on the Fermanagh/Cavan border. Much money is spent in prospecting for new useful rocks.

Fig. 3.9. Peat can be a useful product and, by careful management, the land can be restored to profitable use as farmland. Will that improve the landscape?

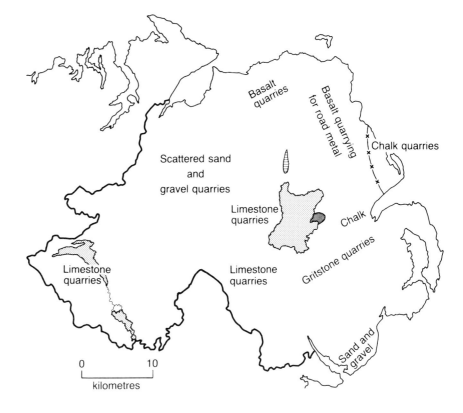

Fig. 3.10. Present use of rocks in Northern Ireland.

Key
- Diatomite
- Lignite
- ×—×— West boundary of salt field

Problem: Quality

Is what has been found good enough for use?
Clay of the Triassic age was good enough for making bricks to build houses in Belfast in the nineteenth century (quarried on Black Mountain). For fire-bricks, it was necessary to use the quartz-rich Carboniferous clays found at Coalisland. Nowadays, clay formed from the skeletons of microscopic creatures is mined in the Lower Bann Valley for insulation materials. Any natural resource must be of the right quality to be useful.

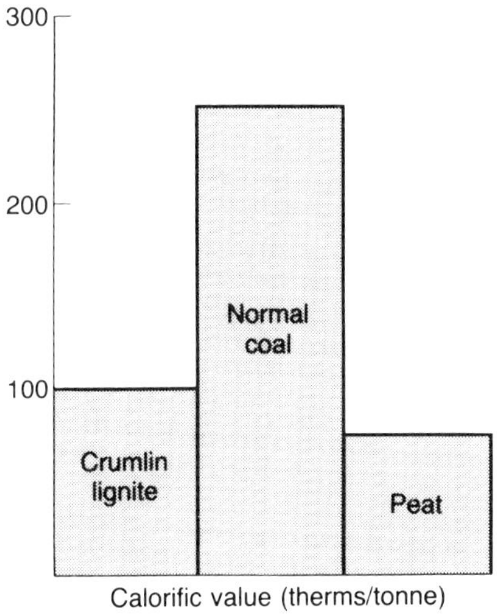

Problem: The market

Can the product be sold?
There is plenty of sandstone, but no market for sandstone blocks nowadays for public building. There are massive salt deposits near Larne, but the market is limited. Limestone and chalk can however be sold from the many quarries for cement manufacture and fertilisers. The market changes with the state of the economy and technology.

Problem: Distance

Is the market near enough?
Bauxite, found in the weathered layers between the basalt flows in County Antrim, was once exported to make aluminium in Scotland. There are still large reserves here, but they lie deep beneath 750 metres of basalt. Transporting it would also be expensive, so further exploitation is unlikely. A little is used for filters in sewage plants.

Fig. 3.11. Calorific values of solid fuels.

(Bar chart showing calorific values in therms/tonne: Crumlin lignite ≈ 100, Normal coal ≈ 250, Peat ≈ 75)

Problem: Capital costs

Can we afford it?

Lignite deposits may be mined near Crumlin and Ardboe but it would cost too much to transport the lignite any distance because of its low value (fig. 3.11). Most of it will be used to fuel a new power station nearby. The Government has to make decisions about alternative energy sources, for example that Kilroot power station should be changed from oil to coal burning, whether natural gas should be piped from Kinsale or Scotland, or should renewable sources such as tidal power or wind power be harnessed? Each scheme depends on huge capital investment.

More modest investments are made by individuals or small firms, for example in simple machines to extract peat from bogs between Omagh and Cookstown for direct sale for domestic heating and for garden compost (figs. 3.9 and 3.12).

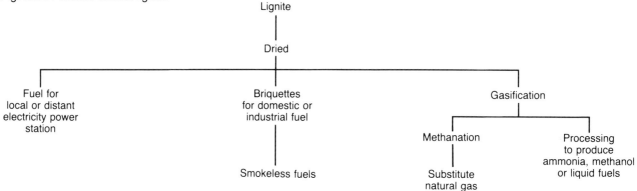

Fig. 3.12. Possible uses of lignite.

Problem: Pollution and dereliction

Are social costs too high?

Mining and quarrying can have a marked effect on the environment. The chalk quarries at Larry Bane Head, for example, were a serious blot on the beautiful north coast near Ballintoy. Clay quarries at Coalisland left scenes of dereliction. Exploration in Fermanagh and Donegal for uranium gave rise to fears of radiation.

The social costs of mining have to be paid by someone. It is always difficult to decide whether we as a community should pay the price of pollution so that natural resources can be exploited for profit; or should we insist that the landscape be restored after exploitation at the risk of putting off those willing to make an investment?

Exercises

1. Look back at fig. 1.3 on p. 6. The River Faughan 'changes its mind' when only 2 km from the River Foyle. This river diversion was due to a large glacier persisting in the main valley. The River Faughan, swollen with meltwater, was unable to join the River Foyle, so it formed a new channel. It now joins the estuary 8 km to the north. The Burn Dennet had the same problem but later managed to reach the River Foyle by a more direct route. Its old valley is occupied by the misfit Burngibbagh.

Fig. 3.13. The River Bush: its present course.

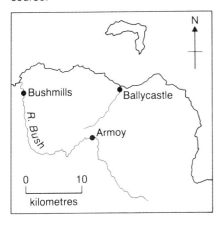

Fig. 3.14. Can Slieve Donard experience another ice age?

Try to explain a similar diversion of the River Bush (fig. 3.13).
2. Study fig. 3.7 which shows some features of the Northern Ireland climate.
   (a) Name the two districts experiencing the lowest mean minimum January temperature. Try to explain this distribution.
   (b) What are the coolest areas in July during the daytime? How can you explain this?
   (c) How can you account for the distribution of gales? Remember that for about 270 days of the year, winds blow from the south-west quadrant and that winds generally are stronger over the flat sea than over more uneven land surfaces. Comment on the importance of gales to the province's ports (refer to pages 85–7).
   (d) Comment on the distribution of fog in relation to the situations of Aldergrove and Belfast Harbour airports.
3. Slieve Donard, the highest mountain in Northern Ireland, is 852 metres high. If fig. 3.14 is accepted as indicating the present height of the snowline in the northern hemisphere, how many metres is Slieve Donard short of having a permanent ice-cap again? How far south would the Arctic ice have to be before Slieve Donard was ice-capped? Using your knowledge of world climatic conditions, criticise this model.

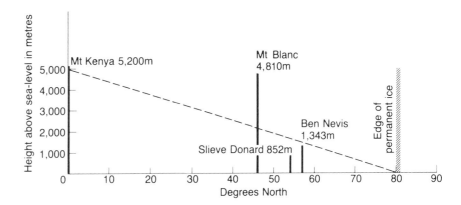

4. A power station has a life of about twenty-five years. It would take up to ten years to plan and build one. Perhaps the lignite on the east shore of Lough Neagh could be delivered to an existing power station which could be redesigned to burn lignite. A constant supply of lignite would be essential; this may mean 5,000 tonnes a day when demand for electricity is high.
   The alternative routes could be as follows:
   (i) By barge down the River Bann to Coleraine. It may then be possible to pipe it in slurry form to Coolkeeragh power station (which at present burns oil).
   (ii) By lorry to:
       (a) West Bank power station near Belfast docks, or
       (b) Ballylumford, near Larne, or
       (c) Kilroot, near Carrickfergus.
       (a) burns coal; (b) burns oil; (c) did burn oil but is being converted to coal.
   (iii) By train to:
       (a) Kilroot via Antrim and Greenisland, or
       (b) Ballylumford via Larne and a new bridge.
   Write a consultant's report to the Northern Ireland Electricity Board, stating whether you would recommend them to move the lignite to a power station, giving reasons. If it proves necessary, explain how the lignite should be transported. (You will need to draw sketch map(s).)

4 People on the land

ecosystem
The term used to describe a natural system, fuelled by the sun's energy, in which living and non-living factors react and are kept in equilibrium.
This ecosystem (fig. 4.1) normally provides free heat, light, moisture and soil for the farmer.

Fig. 4.1. The ecosystem.

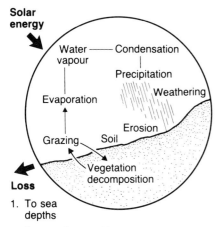

Loss
1. To sea depths
2. Export of vegetable matter

A farmer's wife goes to the shops for meat and groceries like everyone else. She no longer depends on the food produced on the farm. Indeed farming is now an industry, not just a way of life. Sometimes we hear the term 'factory farm'. Is a farm just a kind of food factory?

In a factory, production can be started or stopped whenever necessary. It is under the control of those who manage and work there. Farming has to take account of the natural world, where everything goes on relentlessly and cannot be stopped, started or fundamentally changed. We call this natural world an **ecosystem** (figs. 4.1 and 4.2).

Each farmer has to make choices about such things as seeds, stock and machinery. Economic forces influence his decisions. For instance, if the farmer is to make a profit he must consider the price he is going to get for his products. Prices depend on how many other farmers, here or abroad, produce the same goods. If too much is for sale at any time, the price has to be dropped to encourage customers to buy more. Farmers are more affected by fluctuating prices than factory managers. Often they must sell quickly and cannot store their perishable products nor suddenly slow down production.

There are other economic factors. For a few products a farmer is guaranteed a fixed selling price by the EEC. Grants may be given to improve the land. Regulations are made to control the spread of diseases. The rate of interest the banks charge for any loans needed to develop new aspects of the business is very important.

Every farmer considers the constraints of the ecosystem and the economic influences. Then he himself has to decide between different farming activities, different kinds of seed and breed and whether to invest in new machinery. How much effort he wants to put into his farm may depend on whether he is one of the province's many part-time farmers. So all farms in Northern Ireland will be different from each other. Fig. 4.3 is a model which may be used to help to describe and explain any farm you choose to study.

A sample farm

As you read the following description of a particular farm, think of how the facts fit in to the model.

The farm of 22 hectares is in drumlin country, near Keady, south Armagh. The slopes are too steep in places for ploughing. The fields between the hills are boggy. Much of the soil is waterlogged but there are patches of fertile and reasonably flat land. There grass for silage-making or a good potato crop can be grown. Cattle graze on the rest of the farm.

This farmer milks twenty Friesian dairy cows twice a day. Until recently the milking buckets were emptied into a large cooling tank on wheels. This had to be trundled to the farm entrance once a day and emptied by the tanker lorry from the Armagh creamery. Since 1983 all

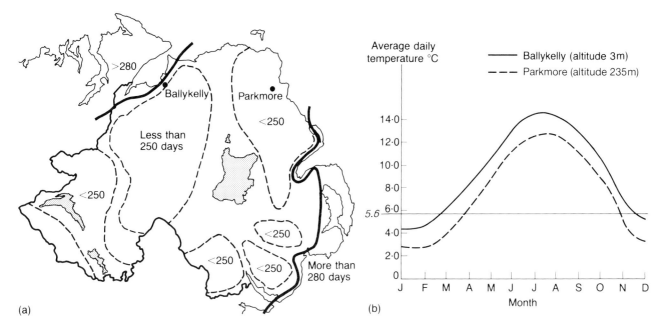

Fig. 4.2. The growing season in Northern Ireland:
(a) The growing season is the period when the mean daily temperature is greater than 5.6°C.
(b) The effect of altitude on the growing season.
Give a name to each of the most favoured areas in Northern Ireland. What advantages will farmers in those areas have? Will a temperature below 5.6°C affect cattle farmers as much as arable farmers? Can you account for the distribution of the less-favoured areas?

Fig. 4.3 A model of the influences on a farmer.

milk from the province's farms has been collected direct from bulk tanks owned or rented by the farmer. There is only room for eight cows in his byre so each milking takes about an hour. The farmer keeps most of the calves that are born on the farm, either to add to his herd or to fatten for beef. At times he may have as many as twenty calves and twenty more cattle being fattened. Sometimes he sells a few in the Keady market. He makes a lot of silage in spring and early summer to feed cattle in the winter when they are kept in the sheds. He also has to buy cattle nuts which contain extra minerals for winter feed.

The farmer has nine breeding sows each producing two litters of about eleven pigs a year. These piglets are sold locally and will eventually be fattened by some other farmer and sold to the bacon factory.

The growth of grass for grazing and silage is encouraged by adding artificial fertiliser. Pig and cattle manure is spread in April and October. Seed potatoes are bought each year; about half a hectare is planted and the crop is sold locally.

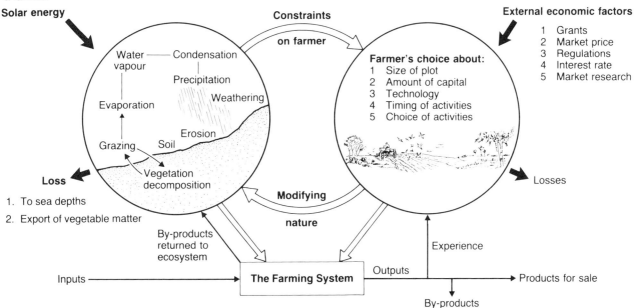

Because this farm, like many others in Northern Ireland, produces several different items, we call it a mixed farm.

How farmers are influenced

The influence of the government is particularly strong in dairy farming. It was found that milk helped to spread disease, particularly of tuberculosis. Regulations were introduced to ensure regular inspection of animal health and strict hygienic conditions for milking and pasteurisation of the milk. Farmers in return needed to be sure of getting a regular income for their milk. In Northern Ireland the Milk Marketing Board buys all of it at a fixed price. This encouraged many farmers in Northern Ireland to become specialist dairy farmers, using much advanced technology and expert management to reduce costs and improve yields. One such farm is described in Table 4. Europe also began to produce more and more milk each year, too much for the Continent to use (fig. 4.4). In 1984 EEC quotas for each country were fixed and each farmer in Northern Ireland had to reduce his output by 9%. To do this he had to sell milking cows at a time when everyone else was doing the same.

Fig. 4.4. Milk production in Northern Ireland:
(a) How our milk was used in 1984.
(b) Milk production in 1977 and 1983.

What effect would this have on the selling price?

(a)

From the farms

Milk Marketing Board
1,418 million litres

Liquid sales
14.5% at
20.6p per litre

Used for manufacture
85.5% at 14.3p per litre

Full-price milk 13.8%

Butter 54.6%

Cheese 19.9%

Whole milk powder 6.5%

Cream, etc. 4.4%

Welfare milk 0.7%

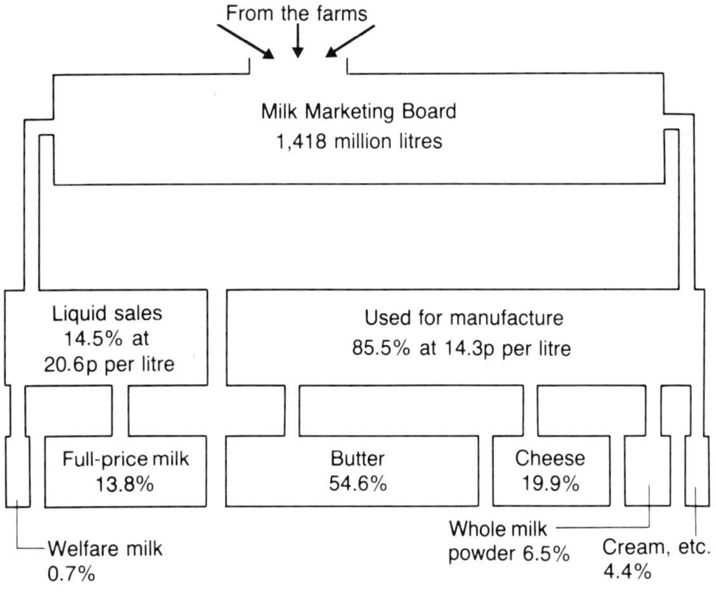

(b)

	1977	1983
Total output of milk (million litres)	1,056	1,416
Number of dairy cows (thousands)	248	291
Yield per cow (litres)	4,291	4,870

The influence of the EEC on pig-rearing is very different: it has affected pig farmers mostly through the cost of foodstuffs. Before the days of the EEC, grains imported from America were roughly the same price for Irish or any other European pig farmers. The EEC decided to support cereal growers in Europe by heavily taxing imports of grain. Prices of animal foodstuffs imported for Irish farmers then became much higher than the prices paid by pig farmers in cereal-growing parts of Europe. In Northern Ireland, only specialist farmers can now make a good living from pigs, though keeping a few pigs is still important on a very small farm (fig. 4.5).

Table 4 *A specialist dairy farm in County Antrim.*

Size	75 hectares (43 owned and 32 rented annually by conacre agreement)
Herd	75 Friesian cows 90 others (on average)
Crops	All grass, producing 800 tonnes of silage (as well as summer grazing)
Extra cattle feed	Cattle nuts (the exact amount, to suit the state of the animal, is controlled by a computer; each cow is recognised by a 'responder' on its collar) Average feed 0.3 kg per day per litre of milk produced
Average milk production of the herd	412,000 litres a year (output of each cow is recorded by computer)
Other outputs	50 calves sent to market (plus 20 retained in herd) 15 cull cows sent to market Slurry

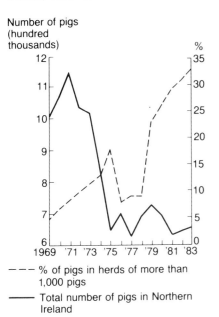

Fig. 4.5. Pig production in Northern Ireland, 1969–83.

– – – % of pigs in herds of more than 1,000 pigs

—— Total number of pigs in Northern Ireland

Potato-growing in Northern Ireland is widespread and is mainly for the home market. Here there is no fixed price; before they plant, farmers have to guess what the weather is going to be, what size their crop is likely to be, and what price they will get per kilo sold. After a high-price year, farmers tend to plant more and the price therefore falls the following year. To ensure a more steady income, some choose to specialise in seed potatoes for export where the price usually varies less from year to year.

A real factory farm?

A farmer can only hope to escape from the influence of the ecosystem by working indoors.

Mushrooms used to be grown on trays in a large, heated, well-ventilated building, often in the dark. Soil had to be specially cleaned because the artificial climate (very moist and warm) favoured the growth of many kinds of bacteria, some of which would ruin the mushrooms.

Had the farmer really escaped from the ecosystem? And had the grower escaped the economic influences? Looking at Table 5, can you account for the disappearance from production of many Northern Irish mushroom farmers between 1972 and 1978, the years when oil prices rose steeply? Do the figures justify the conclusion that only by specialising in bigger production units were farmers able to stay in business (nearly half the output in the province is now produced by the ten largest growers)?

Table 5 *Trends in the production of mushrooms in Northern Ireland.*

	1972	1978	1983
No. of growers	219	128	130
Production (million kg)	5.5	3.2	4.6
Size of holdings (% of total number)			
0–500 m²	51	39	35
>1,500 m²	7	17	22

Fig. 4.6. Most mushrooms are grown in bags in simple buildings. Compost is sterilised in the factories and sold in sealed polythene bags already spawned. The high-density compost generates heat, helping to maintain a temperature of about 24°C for 2–3 weeks. The grower then opens the bags and adds a top layer (5 cm) of a mixture of peat and lime. The temperature is allowed to drop gradually to 17°C but humidity has to be kept very high despite ventilating to remove carbon dioxide. Three weeks later, cropping starts and lasts for five weeks.

Two-thirds of mushroom growers are in County Armagh, and some are also fruit growers or horticulturalists. Nearly 70% of production is exported to Great Britain (mainly Glasgow, Liverpool and Manchester); only a very small amount is frozen or canned.

Nowadays, to reduce heating costs mushrooms are grown in insulated buildings in bags of compost in which the spores have been planted in the factory (fig. 4.6).

How does this reduce the farmer's costs (consider capital, running and labour costs)?

'Factory farming' techniques are not limited to mushroom growing. Chickens are kept in batteries of cages. Farmers are provided with the birds from a commercial hatchery. The farmer supervises the birds, controlling their food supply, the heating and lighting (providing an artificial day and night). The products (poultry for slaughter, or eggs) are bought at a guaranteed price.

Pigs and cattle can similarly be kept indoors, fed and watered under strict control. As many as 300 cattle can be kept on one hectare. By this method, costs can be controlled. As long as the selling price is assured, profits can be increased this way. No one objects to factory farming of mushrooms; some people criticise these practices when applied to animals.

Fig. 4.7. The percentage contribution of each type of farming enterprise to the earnings of the Northern Ireland agricultural industry.

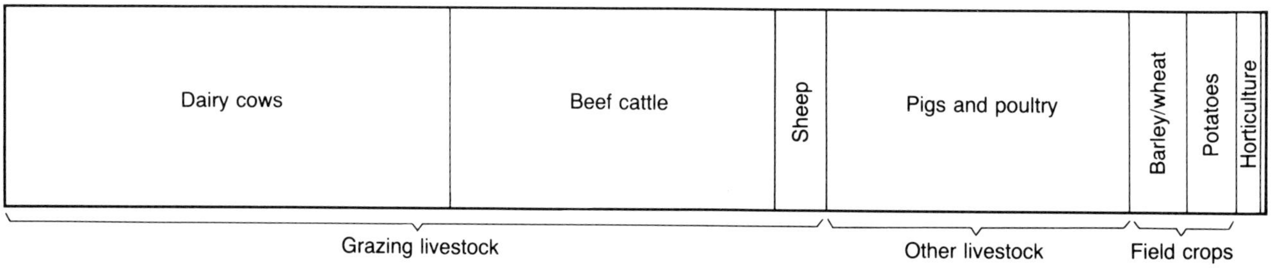

Dairy cows	Beef cattle	Sheep	Pigs and poultry	Barley/wheat	Potatoes	Horticulture

Grazing livestock — Other livestock — Field crops

Look at Table 6 and fig. 4.7 and try to explain (a) why these changes are taking place and (b) why, although the number of farmers is decreasing, the output is increasing. Is there a danger in bigger specialised units? Would smaller diverse units be more easily able to adjust to changes in demand? What are the advantages of specialisation and large-scale production? Is a farm really a food factory nowadays?

Table 6 *Changes in Northern Ireland's farm structure.*

	1976	1977	1978	1979	1980	1981	1982	1983	1984
Agricultural labour force (thousands)	67.8	65.8	65.7	64.7	63.5	60.7	60.3	60.8	60.5
Number of farm businesses[1]	32,629	32,352	31,715	31,075	27,118	26,027	25,542	25,461	25,489
Number of larger holdings[2]	4,993	5,120	5,262	5,371	2,699	2,690	2,794	2,914	3,042
Gross Output Index[3]	82.3	93.8	100.0	98.4	102.6	101.5	104.0	109.5	113.0

[1] These include part-time and full-time businesses but exclude very small holdings (i.e. less than 50 standard man-days up to 1979 and less than 1 European Standard Unit from 1980). Adjustments have been made to take account of the conacre (seasonal letting) system.
[2] These refer to businesses classified as greater than 600 standard man-days (greater than 16 European Standard Units from 1980).
[3] This is calculated at constant prices, using 1978 as the base.

Fig. 4.8. Northern Ireland's recreational areas. It is said that most people will only travel about 40 km for a day visit to a park; very few will travel more than 80 km. Does this explain which parks you haven't visited? How would you set about testing whether these statements are true?

Key
- • Department of Environment Country Park
- Department of Agriculture Forest Park
- Area of Outstanding Natural Beauty
- Proposed Area of Outstanding Natural Beauty

Forestry

Northern Ireland has over 14,000 km² of land, but activities besides farming compete for it. For example, the forest authority in Northern Ireland owns over 73,000 hectares. No forest produces anything of value for sale before it is twenty years old. Profits will not come until the next century. Even foresters avoid very long-term investments. Oak, beech and other hardwood trees grow too slowly. Mostly Sitka spruce and Lodgepole pine are planted; they can be harvested in about sixty years.

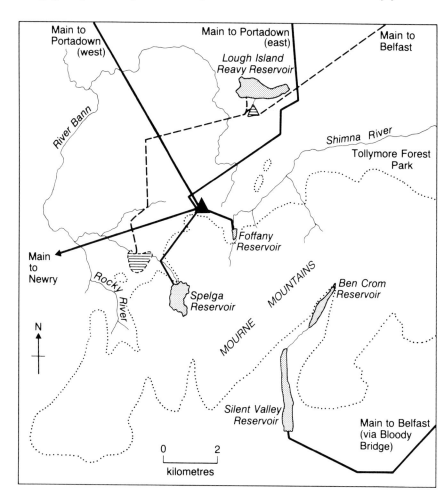

Fig. 4.9. Kinnahalla Water Scheme.

Key
— Water main
▲ Treatment works
Proposed Kinnahalla reservoir and pipelines
·········· 300m contour line

(a) Comparison of Tunny Point and Kinnahalla schemes

	Tunny Point	Kinnahalla
Capital cost	£16m	£18m
Area to be flooded	—	50 hectares
Energy demands	100% of water to be pumped up 100 metres	55% of water to be pumped up 27 metres
Yield	230 million litres/day	115 million litres/day
Cost per day per litre supplied (average)	0.32p	0.28p

(b) Water demand

The demand is 300 litres per person per day. Nearly half of this is used directly in the home:

Flushing lavatory	50 litres
Washing, bathing	50 litres
Laundry	13.5 litres
Washing-up	13.5 litres
Car and garden	9 litres
Drinking and cooking	3 litres

Industry uses water for cooling purposes and in processing: e.g. the manufacture of

1 bag of cement uses	180 litres
1 litre of beer uses	350 litres
1 kg of nylon uses	1,000 litres
1 car tyre uses	190,000 litres

Forests provide timber for building, boxes, paper pulp and chipboard, but there is a good 'by-product': they hold the soil firm on steep slopes; their roots absorb rainwater and release it slowly into the streams.

Thirty years ago it was realised that forests can also provide something else: opportunities for recreation in forest parks (fig. 4.8). Nearly 1 million visits a year are made to these and to other open forest areas. Attempts are made to educate visitors concerning the environment, and by charging for admission more people are employed and more facilities can be provided.

Water supply

By the year 2000, the demand for water in the Greater Belfast area will probably be about 550 million litres per day. From present sources only 410 million litres can be made available. Three schemes were considered to solve the problem, but all would use up some land.

(a) The Glenwhirry scheme involved damming the river above Kells, County Antrim (see fig. 3.4).
(b) The Tunny Point scheme involved extraction of water from Lough Neagh and pumping it up 100 metres on its way to the Belfast area (see fig. 3.4).
(c) The Kinnahalla scheme involved damming the river near Kinnahalla Youth Hostel and piping water to a treatment plant near Lough Island Reavy. Except for the pumping of the additional supply from Lough Island Reavy itself up 27 metres to the plant, the flow would be by gravity to Belfast.

Fig. 4.10. Possible HEP schemes:
(a) River Mourne HEP scheme (output 27.5 MW).
(b) River Bann HEP scheme (output 15.0 MW).
The River Bann scheme would save 15,000 tonnes of oil a year and produce cheap electricity for a very long time. Does this justify flooding the land and the high capital expense?

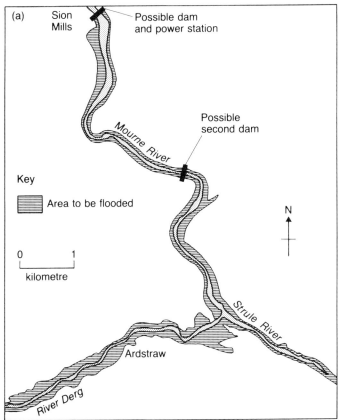
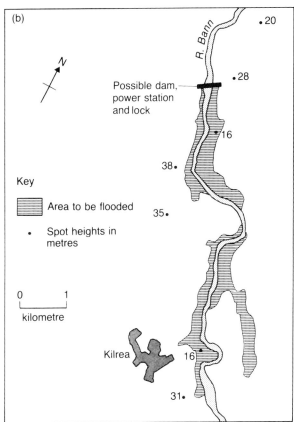

Fig. 4.11. A possible tidal power scheme at Strangford Lough, which covers 144 km² at high tide. The output at a barrage in the narrows, despite the small tidal range, could be 210 MW but it would only be produced for about four hours twice a day while the tide was falling.

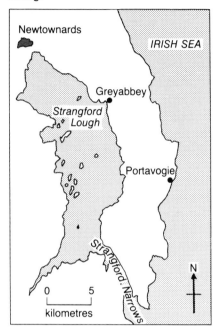

For scheme (a), 380 hectares of agricultural land as well as some dwellings would have to be flooded; it was therefore rejected. Fuel costs for the pumps would make scheme (b) expensive to run. Flooded land in scheme (c) would be almost entirely uninhabited moorland; the new dam would be landscaped and trees planted.

At the public enquiry into the proposal for scheme (c) the following interests were represented: (a) Youth Hostel Association (b) Fisheries Conservancy Board (c) Public Health Committee (d) Ulster Farmers Union (e) Sports Council (f) Ulster Architectural Heritage Society (g) Ulster Society for Preservation of Countryside (h) various angling clubs.

Arguments concerned (a) changes in the scenery, (b) changes in pollution levels in the River Bann and the river's ability to cope with these, (c) facilities for sport and field studies, (d) the water requirements after the year 2000, and (e) comparative energy costs.

With the help of fig. 4.9 try to write out a likely submission from each group. Was the enquiry right to reject the scheme? Should we be prepared to use more energy to preserve mountains as they are? Does fig. 4.9 indicate any other way in which demands on land could be reduced?

Hydroelectric power (HEP) generation also sometimes involves flooding agricultural land. Northern Ireland does not have rivers with large volume and significant falls. Two schemes only are considered possible and both involve flooding (see fig. 4.10); either would save oil.

Another way to generate electricity involves using the tidal flow out of Strangford Lough (fig. 4.11).

1. The electricity board must have enough capacity to supply *peak* demand. Why are the times of the tide so significant?
2. Can you think of any way of storing the electricity that would be produced at night when demand is low? (The Camlough Pump Storage scheme at Slieve Gullion was started for this purpose but because of the troubles work stopped in 1972.)
3. How might the changing of the environment affect the very special birdlife on the Lough shores?
4. The cost of construction would be very high, perhaps £500 million. The saving on fossil fuels, after allowing for running costs, could be £25 million per year. Is it worth it?

Alternative uses of land

Farmers' land is not only acquired for forests and flooding. Housing and other buildings use land.

A landowner near an expanding town can make a substantial profit if he sells his land for housebuilding. He may also continue to collect groundrent.

Should this unearned gain be taken away by taxation or others means? How would some other landowners feel when the enforcement of planning regulations to prevent city sprawl denies them their profit? (See p. 54 about the Belfast stopline.)

We also take land for roads. Consider the cost, in hectares, of our very simple motorway network of 112 kilometres. An average of six hectares has to be compulsorily bought for each kilometre of motorway. More is needed at intersections and for road-widening schemes.

Some landowners can exploit the geographical position of their fields (fig. 4.12).

(a) (b)

Fig. 4.12. Use of land: (a) a caravan park; (b) an autowrecker's dump. How does the owner make a profit from the uses of land?

Calculate how much income can be obtained from a two-hectare caravan site if, from 1 June to 31 August there are, on average, 200 campers paying £1 per night. Expenses may be £200 per week. Compare this with the value of the same area of grassland which may produce a net gain of £1,000 per hectare per annum if used for farming. Could the farmer use the land for both purposes?

Reclamation is a way of adding to our stock of land (fig. 4.13). Much of central Belfast and the first wide stretch of the M2 was built on land reclaimed from the River Lagan.

Leisure and land needs

People used to spend their leisure time in town parks which started as gardens or estates of wealthy residents. Can you recognise any in your area? When the railways came, leisure time could be spent at holiday resorts with their promenades and bathing beaches. Nowadays we have even greater mobility with the motor-car. We live in a period of mass leisure.

reclamation
It is possible to reclaim land from rivers or the sea. Reclamation for farmland has been very successful on the coast near the mouth of the River Roe (fig. 4.13). Dykes have been built to keep out the sea. Then the land behind the dykes has been drained and so reclaimed as first-grade agricultural land. Such land is called a 'polder'.

How can planners satisfy modern demands to enjoy broad stretches of countryside? They have to remember:
(a) to protect the environment from overuse or misuse;
(b) that haphazard activity can interfere with farmers and be very wasteful and unsightly;
(c) that tourism as an industry can increase local employment prospects.

The need for developments that stimulate employment and produce wealth have to be balanced against our desire to preserve the traditional landscape as it has been for the past 100 years or more.

Possible strategies are to establish the following:

1. National Parks, administered by a National Park Committee keen on conservation but planning to provide for an increasing number of visitors. It would seek to improve the scenic value, restore natural vegetation and restore buildings. Because of political pressures, no National Parks have been established in Northern Ireland.
2. Areas of Outstanding Natural Beauty. These are managed by local authorities to prevent unsightly development (fig. 4.8).
3. Country Parks, managed by the Department of the Environment, seeking to encourage visitors to concentrate in specific areas (fig. 4.8).
4. National Trust properties, managed by a charity.

Fig. 4.13. Reclamation.

5. Long-distance paths, e.g. the Ulster Way, a 720-km walk around the province which was negotiated with landowners and backed by the Sports Council.
6. Forest Parks, managed by the Department of Agriculture (fig. 4.8).
7. Areas of Special Control. Planning regulations have been relaxed to try to stimulate employment but some areas (e.g. Green Belts around towns) are still thought to need some protection.

The Ulster Lakeland is an area of great tourist potential. A geographer interviewed visitors to Castle Archdale Country Park, using a questionnaire (figs. 4.14 and 4.15). It was noticed that everyone tended to crowd into a small area near the marina and that numbers peaked strongly at certain limited hours (e.g. 2–5 pm on Sundays). This particular survey showed the following:

(a) 57% of visitors came from the Greater Belfast area, 30% came from the local area, 81% were staying overnight.
(b) Overwhelmingly they came for 'peace and quiet', scenery, or fresh air.
(c) Suggestions for improvement and development included: more seats, signposts, a better café, a golfing green, an information centre, boats trips. But most wanted nothing to change; 97% intended to come back for another visit.

Fig. 4.14. Castle Archdale Country Park, County Fermanagh: (a) photograph of marina; (b) map. We say that country parks with their car parks, toilets, nature trails, campsites, etc. have a 'honey-pot' effect. What do you think that means?

Fig. 4.15. A questionnaire used at Castle Archdale Country Park.

Questionnaire

Sex M/F	Age	Accompanied by	Transport	Occupation
	<16	No one	Car	
	17–30	Family	Boat	
Home town	31–60	Friends	Bike	
	>60	Party	Bus	
			Foot	
Why choose this park?	How long will you stay?	Will you visit:	Will you stay overnight in:	
Convenience	<1 hour	Marina	Youth hostel	
Scenery	Most of day	Courtyard	Campsite	
Fresh air	1–3 days	Parkland	Caravan site	
Peace and quiet	4–7 days	Small lakes	Boat	
Activity	>7 days	Forest walk	Not staying overnight	
How many times have you visited here before? What improvements would you suggest? Do you think the park is: overcrowded/just right/under-used/don't know				

Planners hope gradually to persuade visitors to spread more widely over the park, for overcrowding produces problems. Beach B is being developed for barbecues; lakes L are being stocked with ducks. A butterfly garden, arboretum and museum are planned.

1. Visitors can be classed as
   (a) tourists from a distance;
   (b) day-trippers and second-home owners;
   (c) local residents having a day off.
   How will their needs differ?
2. The local authority would like to establish a 'complete holiday destination' to attract tourists on package tours from a distance and even from overseas. Why is that?
3. If this were agreed, which of the items listed below would you recommend for this park and where would you place them?
4. Is there anything on this list which you feel is unsuitable for a country park? What would you add to the list to make it attract 'package tour' visitors from overseas?

Lakeshore promenade
Chalets
Rollerskating rink
Indoor entertainment centre
Boat trips to the islands
Archery
Keep-fit stations
Craft centre
Horse-riding
Indoor swimming pool
Canoe-learners' lake
Horsedrawn carriages for transport

Tourism

Tourism is an industry because it employs people and produces profits. Visitors to Northern Ireland spend nearly £100 million a year here (fig. 4.16). About 1 million travel from overseas or from the Republic (fig. 4.18). We also gain from tourism the friendship and knowledge of people we would not otherwise meet. One book about tourists says 'the countryside of Ulster is a golden egg'. Planners try to persuade us not to break the egg. We could, by allowing brash 'urban' houses to be dotted across rural landscapes. We could tolerate obtrusive industrial buildings on or off farms, and insensitive drainage or flooding schemes. We could reject plans for the organised use of the land which seek to satisfy farmer, tourist and everyone.

Fig. 4.16. Tourism in Northern Ireland: (a) the home area of visitors, 1983; (b) leisure pursuits, 1983.

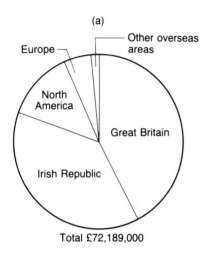
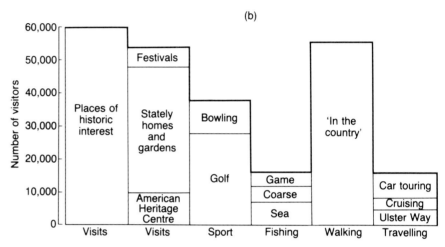

Fig. 4.17. Distribution of different types of farms in Northern Ireland, June 1981.

Key

- A Specialist dairying
- B Other dairying
- C *LFA beef cattle and/or sheep
- D *Non-LFA beef cattle and/or sheep
- E Pigs and/or poultry
- F Mixed livestock
- G Crops and livestock
- H Cropping
- I Horticulture

Number of farms

*Less Favoured Areas are in difficult areas, designated by the EEC for special grants.

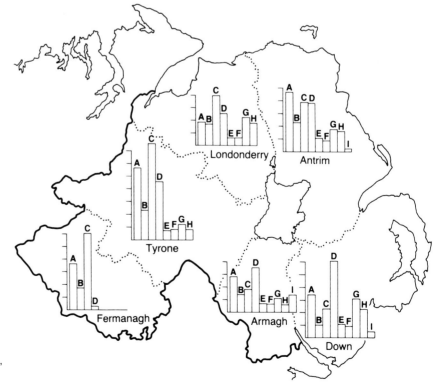

Fig. 4.18. French and German travel brochures for Northern Ireland.

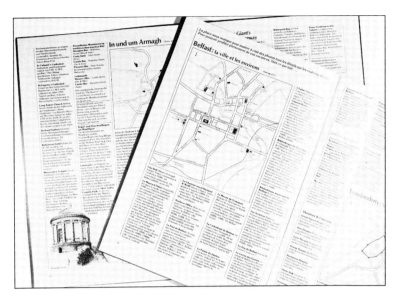

Exercises

1. Here are some quotations from a guidance booklet for Northern Ireland farmers, showing the ways in which the government and the EEC influence farmers' decisions. Decide what each is aiming to do and classify them (a), (b), (c) or (d) according to whether they
   (a) encourage capital development
   (b) ensure fixed prices for products
   (c) attempt to improve quality of products
   (d) control disease.

   (i) 'All sheep must be dipped between 1 October and 30 November each year.'
   (ii) 'Payments are made to speed up conversion to bulk milk collection.'
   (iii) 'Growers are dependent for their returns on the market price supported by intervention-buying in the case of wheat and barley.'
   (iv) 'Seed potatoes may not be offered for sale or shipped unless they qualify for a certificate.'
   (v) 'The guide price for cattle is protected by import levies, customs duties and, when the market price falls, by intervention-buying or aids to private storage.'
   (vi) 'Land improvements in Less Favoured Areas qualify for 50% grants.'
   (vii) 'Grants are available to sheep-flock owners for the purchase of good quality Blackface rams for use in their flock.'

2. In what ways is the farming industry in Northern Ireland (a) different from and (b) similar to a factory industry?

3. From an OS 1:10,000 map of your nearest motorway junction, calculate the area of land used. Relate your answer to the average size of an Irish farm (18 hectares).

4. 'We cannot sanction . . . the preservation of natural beauty spots that would appear to doom large areas . . . to be nothing more than showpieces for the visitor and cheap recreation centres for the holiday maker' (*Hansard* 50, No. 3, 507). Write a parliamentary reply to counter this speech in Stormont in 1967.

5. Study fig. 4.17. Comment on the following:
   (a) The climatic influence on farm types G and H.
   (b) The geographical influence on type I farms in Counties Antrim and Down. What accounts for the larger number of type I farms in Armagh?
   (c) What must be the main crop grown in the fields of farm types A, B, C and D?
   (d) Why are all farms in Fermanagh classified A, B, C or D?

5 Human landscapes

When we are asked where we live, most of us refer to the nearest town to our home. If we are planning a journey we list the towns we shall be passing through. Most of our schools are in towns to which pupils travel daily. Towns seem to dominate our lives; 70% of us live in towns.

Belfast, with the adjoining towns of Lisburn, Bangor and Newtownabbey, obviously dominates Northern Ireland. If all the area between those places becomes built up, we should call it the Belfast conurbation (a continuous town). There are also three other large towns with populations between 30,000 and 60,000.

Can you name them? They are spaced far apart, in the north-west, the north-east and the south of the province (though you may want to argue as to whether Craigavon can yet be regarded as one town incorporating Portadown and Lurgan).

If we say that second-class towns have 10,000–30,000 people, then we can count nine more settlements, such as Larne, Newry and Enniskillen. Places with 3,000–10,000 people (e.g. Ballycastle, Dungannon, Kilkeel) would add twenty-three to our list. There would be even more smaller towns with a population of 1,000 to 3,000 such as Castlederg, Eglinton and Crossmaglen. Together this system forms a **hierarchy**.

Fig. 5.2 shows the different-sized towns in one area of Northern Ireland. Can you see a pattern in the distribution? Consider the distance, on average, between towns. There are some gaps in the pattern. Can you explain them? Are there any settlements in those gaps (an Ordnance Survey map would help you to find out)? These have been omitted from the sketch because they have a population of just under 1,000 people. Are these smaller places really towns? If they act as a market for local people with shops and services such as a chemist, a hardware shop, a solicitor or library, then we could argue that they *are* towns, even if a settlement of similar size in Great Britain would be called a village.

Another reason for the gaps in the pattern can be guessed if you find out what kind of land lies between Maghera and Dungiven, or between Garvagh and Limavady.

This pattern of settlements is repeated all over the province but you may find it a challenge to explain gaps in the pattern near your area.

The size of the town is related to its function. The larger the town the more **high-order goods and services** it offers and the greater the distance people are prepared to travel to obtain them. A shopkeeper who sells such goods and services needs to be within reach of a large number of customers, for he will not expect any one family to buy his 'luxury' goods very often. The line on the map encloses an area where according to one geographer at least 80% of the residents would shop for clothes in Ballymena. This area is called the 'urban field' of Ballymena. Using other purchases such as wholesale groceries or furniture, or using the distribution area for local newspapers, the urban field may be slightly different. Every town has an urban field even if only, in the case of the very small towns, for **low-order goods**.

---

hierarchy
An arrangement with a few most important things at the top and numerous less important items at the bottom. Fig. 5.1 arranges towns in Northern Ireland in a hierarchy according to size.

Fig. 5.1. The hierarchy of towns in Northern Ireland.

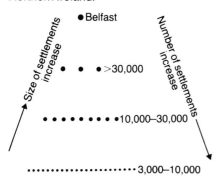

---

high- and low-order goods and services
Low-order goods are those for which we need to shop frequently, e.g. newspapers, milk, bread. High-order goods and services are those we require only occasionally, e.g. antiques, estate agents, furniture.

So the pattern has these characteristics:
(a) Settlements tend to be evenly distributed.
(b) Each settlement has its own 'field' or sphere of influence.
(c) There is a hierarchy of settlement, the number of small settlements being greater than the number of large ones and being interspersed among them.

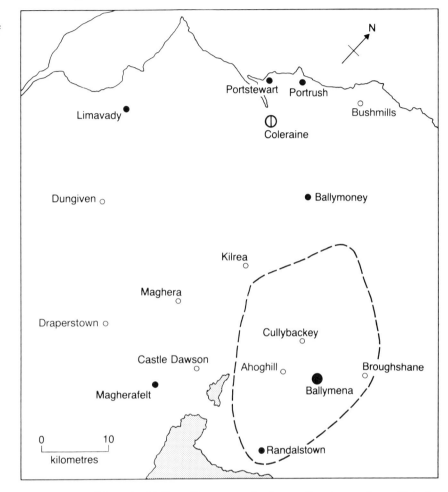

Fig. 5.2. The distribution of towns with more than 1,000 inhabitants in a part of County Antrim and Londonderry.

Key

Population size (thousands)

● 30–60   1st class

◐ 10–30   2nd class

• 3–10   3rd class

○ 1–3   4th class

– – – Urban field of Ballymena

Fig. 5.3. The remnants of a clachan settlement in County Down, with modern bungalows attracted by the seaside location.

Bus timetables, the Yellow Pages or telephone directory, places listed in local newspaper advertisements and reports, the catchment area of your school – all these may help you to draw the urban field or the hierarchy of settlement in your area.

How did this pattern develop?

Phase A (before about AD 1100). People used to live in low houses made from local materials (rock, mud, turf, timber and thatch) scattered over the countryside. In places they were grouped together with others occupied by their kinsmen to make a 'clachan' (fig. 5.3). There was little need to trade: it was subsistence living. There were no towns, though Armagh and Downpatrick were monastic settlements with occasional fairs.

Phase B. When abbeys and castles were established, market stalls were often set up nearby. Without protection, markets were very vulnerable to raiders. Communication by water was a great help to trade, especially beyond the Irish coast. Carrickfergus and Newry were established in this phase (fig. 5.4).

Phase C. In plantation times (1600 and later), town building was deliberately organised and planned, based on experience on the mainland. Careful thought was given to defence as well as to trade. Amongst those towns founded were Limavady, Strabane, Charlemont, Mountjoy, Coleraine, Enniskillen and Dungannon. In the more peaceful eighteenth century, some energetic landowners devised more towns with impressive central squares such as Hillsborough, Castlewellan, Warrenpoint, Newtownards and, on rather a different plan, Draperstown (see fig. 5.5). Many smaller unplanned market centres grew up at crossroads or river crossings.

Fig. 5.4. An early sketch of Carrickfergus.

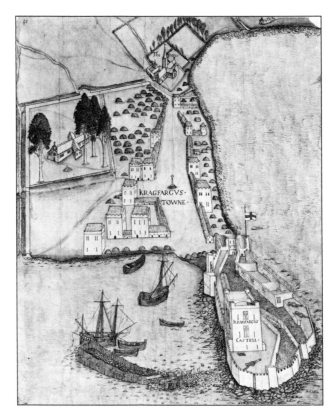

Fig. 5.5. The Drapers' Company had this settlement planned and built in the period up to 1840. The triangular green, lined with trees, served as a fairground. A market house, hotel, dispensary and churches were included in the design. This photograph shows the centre of Draperstown today.

Phase D. In the late nineteenth century, some towns grew very quickly, while some stagnated.
The differences can be related to several factors:
(a) The building of the railways, e.g. Portadown thrived because it became the main railway junction on the Belfast / Dublin line. Armagh had no such stimulus.
(b) Industry in the larger towns attracted people from the rural areas. Rows of terrace houses were built around the factories (fig. 5.6). Eventually health problems led to legislation on the minimum standards of houses, but big towns still grew faster than small ones.
(c) Some towns grew because of their attraction for visitors, e.g. Portrush. Previously it had been an outport for Coleraine which for a time had been handicapped by a sandbar across the mouth of the River Bann.

Phase E. In the first half of the twentieth century trams and the

Fig. 5.6. Hilden Mill and houses, near Lisburn.

gentrification
The improvement and refitting to a high standard of old houses in certain desirable areas of inner cities.

Radburn planning
Attempting to separate pedestrian and cycle paths from traffic roads.

Fig. 5.7. 'Yes, we think the government built these BMX tracks in the early 1980s – but what "BMX" stands for . . . search me!'

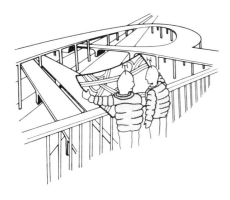

Sea wrack
A type of edible seaweed which was particularly valuable in wintertime when animal fodder was scarce.

motor-car were introduced. Towns began to sprawl, for people could travel longer distances to work. Growth was unplanned and uncontrolled. Agricultural land was taken over. Houses were built along either side of the main roads spreading out from the towns; this is called ribbon development. Factories now powered by electricity could disperse to suburban sites. Villages were engulfed by the urban spread.

Phase F. In the last half of this century there have been attempts to restrict the sprawl of towns. Inner cities are being redeveloped or rehabilitated, and houses **gentrified**. Some houses are being remodelled into 'town houses' for those who can afford a second home in the country or by the sea. **Radburn-type planning** is common. Problems arising from congestion, pollution and disposal of rubbish have not yet been solved.

Phase G. The next stage, in the future, may reflect
(a) the exhaustion of the world's oil supplies and possibly the limited range of electric cars;
(b) heating costs which might drive towns underground to conserve heat supplied by solar panels above;
(c) microelectronics communications and control which could significantly reduce the need to centralise activities in factories and offices; much work may be done from home by telecommunications and robots.

You may be able to think of other influences that could alter the pattern of settlement. The tendency to build supermarkets outside towns is already presenting new planning problems.

What might happen if we abandoned planning altogether?

An example of the pattern developing

On the north coast of County Down, before the sixteenth century, there was only one significant centre of occupation: the monastery at Bangor. Virtually nothing of it remains today. The Anglo-Normans who built castles at Carrickfergus and Strangford had no foothold on this coast. The few inhabitants lived in scattered dwellings in the woods (e.g. in Holle Wood, today's Holywood).

In 1606, very industrious Scottish settlers were introduced and encouraged to build houses. By 1616 a Donaghadee–Portpatrick (Scotland) ferry had been established and a pier built so that **sea wrack** and cattle could be exported and cloth imported. By 1620 permission had been granted to make Bangor a port too. (The only other port nearby was Carrickfergus; Belfast was insignificant in those days.) Bangor's market dates from this time and survives today.

Donaghadee thrived as a port. A packet steamer service continued for 200 years until 1850. There was little difference between the population sizes of Bangor and Donaghadee in 1836. Groomsport never became a real port (except for smuggling), although William of Orange's army landed there in 1689.

In 1865 the Belfast–Bangor railway was opened. Bangor grew quickly as a holiday resort and as a dormitory and residential area. The port aspect became less important except for importing coal; now it is famous for leisure boating of many kinds. Donaghadee (with a population of 3,800) survives as a small port for fishing trips.

Fig. 5.8. The North Down coastal towns.

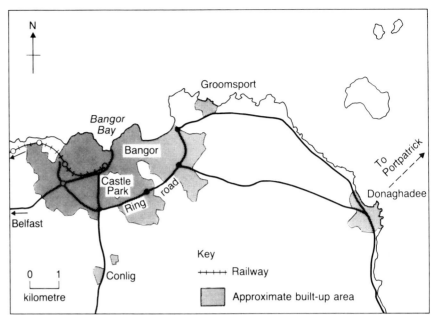

Now in the 'car' age, Bangor (population 46,500) has exploded, with suburbs bursting even beyond the ring road and spawning little commuter estates onto local villages such as Conlig (fig. 5.8).

Can you trace similar stages in the development of settlement in the area where you live?

Fig. 5.9. Londonderry. Foyle Bridge has only recently been opened. Geographers will be watching the changes which result. Will it just be part of a ring road to reduce the city-centre congestion? Will it simply give residents on the west bank easier access to hospitals, industries, etc. on the east bank? Will the residential pattern change? Will industrial location be affected?

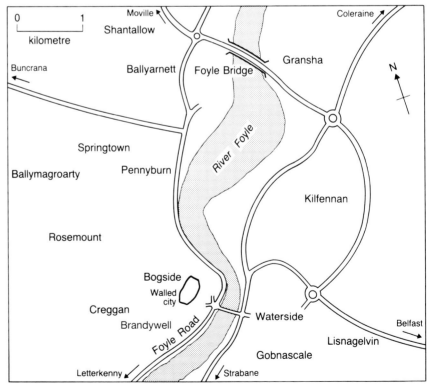

Redeveloping a town: Derry

There were some scattered settlements and a monastery in the Derry region for a thousand years before the plantation of Ulster. The fortified

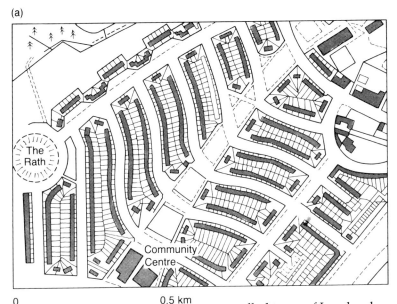

	Persons per hectare	Dwellings per hectare
Older inner city	400	150
New Town	130	40
Affluent suburb	60	20
Modern high-density inner city	300	80

Fig. 5.10. Planning: (a) Creggan. (b) Ballymagroarty. Ballymagroarty was designed 25 years after Creggan. What differences regarding provision for open space and recreation, separation of pedestrian and vehicular traffic, and shopping facilities can you find? (c) Typical housing density figures in Northern Ireland.

walled town of Londonderry was built in the early seventeenth century. The first bridge across the River Foyle in 1790 encouraged development towards the river and the Waterside beyond (fig. 5.9).

In the nineteenth century the city became a centre for shirt-making, distilling and tanning. Industry and commerce were encouraged by the expanding port and the building of four railway networks to the city. 'Back-to-back' terrace houses were built in the Bogside, Rossville Street, the Fountain and Foyle Road to accommodate migrant workers. Their numbers were swollen by the 1847 famine.

In 1946 the Londonderry Corporation began planning for 3,000 dwellings in Creggan Estate to house the growing population and ease overcrowding. There were also housing developments on the outskirts of the city including Glen Road (Rosemount), Gobnascale and Lisnagelvin. The inner city residential area, now over 100 years old, continued to deteriorate. Urgent action was needed.

How would you have tackled this problem? Here are two alternatives:
Strategy 1: Build high-rise flats to house many people. Then demolish the old houses and rebuild at a lower density per hectare.
Strategy 2: Develop more housing estates outside the city. Clear the old areas and redevelop with higher-standard houses, taking account of car requirements, leisure needs, separation of industry and housing.

What are the advantages and disadvantages of each? Think of such factors as
- the long blight during redevelopment
- the break-up of neighbour relationships
- travelling expenses from distant estates
- opportunities to provide or redesign services (electricity, roads, sewers, open spaces)
- psychological upset amongst the elderly.

The Housing Authority first adopted strategy 1 in the Lecky Road/Rossville Street area. Rossville flats were built in 1966, ten storeys high, on the site of a former cattle market; other new dwellings were conventional two-storey houses and maisonettes. Then the policy was changed to the second strategy: 2,500 houses were built in the new suburbs of Shantallow/Ballyarnett outside the city boundary. Since then, Ballymagroarty has also been developed with 650 houses (fig. 5.10).

Meantime Lecky Road/Barrack Street redevelopment (Brandywell) is being achieved by a third strategy, a 'small stages' scheme. About thirty houses at a time are dealt with, with tenants moving easily from old to adjacent new houses. It is a slow method but it helps to maintain community spirit.

Another alternative in urban or rural renewal is to rehabilitate property by means of improvement and repair grants. This method can apply to both public and privately-owned houses and it encourages everyone in a district to maintain his property. Many parts of the city have benefited from this strategy.

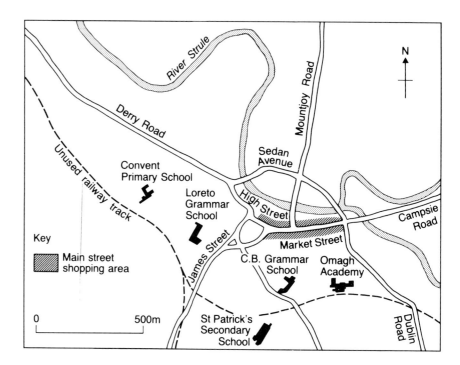

Fig. 5.11. Omagh.

Other planning problems

Planners only have limited powers. They cannot anticipate or resist economic and political forces, new technologies, population growth, changing fashions in living styles. Yet they have to plan for a distant future.

Consider the traffic congestion anticipated even in 1970. For example, an obvious solution to avoid the use of the main streets of Omagh by through traffic is to convert an old unused railway track into a throughpass (fig. 5.11).

Will city traders be happy to see traffic diverted from the centre or will commerce be helped by easier access to new parking areas near the town centre?

Another plan would be to pedestrianise the main shopping area. This involves making it possible to stock shops and serve banks from back streets. Extensive car parking nearby is also needed for shoppers.

What compromise may be possible to relieve the main street from traffic during shopping hours?

The planners in your town probably face difficulties dealing with similar problems. Consider the alternatives that could be adopted, bearing in mind the financial and social costs involved.

Rural settlement

Across most of Northern Ireland, rural houses are widely spaced. There are relatively few real villages (fig. 5.12). It is not uncommon to come across a church or a pub on an isolated site serving a large area of dispersed farms. This contrasts with other parts of the United Kingdom where villages are common and dispersed houses less frequent. The reasons for the difference include the following:

- Water supply from wells and streams was available almost anywhere. Houses did not have to cluster around springs, or alternatively around dry-points in over-watered areas.
- In England, the village pattern was established as early as feudal times, and has persisted; the enclosing of fields was fairly recent. Most farmers are tenants of big farms on long leases; they employ workers who live in villages. In Northern Ireland rural depopulation after the 1840s famine was accompanied by Land Acts which encouraged farmers to own and live on their own smaller holdings of land, turning it into pasture.
- The inheritance tradition of splitting up a farm between the heirs, instead of passing it on complete to the eldest son, has helped in the past to produce smaller farms.

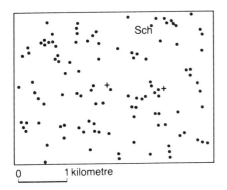

Key
- • House
- Sch School
- + Church

Fig. 5.12. Distribution of rural housing. Notice the distribution of houses, school and churches. What is the average distance between the houses?

There are *some* examples of true villages, designed and built in the eighteenth and early nineteenth centuries. Caledon (County Tyrone) was remodelled after the local mansion had been reconstructed in 1812 following plans by the famous architect Nash. Gracehill (County Antrim) was built in the eighteenth century by the Moravians from Central Europe. Bessbrook (County Armagh) was the first industrial garden village in the British Isles; it was associated with the flax spinning mill. Its planning in 1846 influenced other experiments on the mainland. Eglinton (County Londonderry) was improved around 1821 by the London Company of Grocers with a broad treelined main street and some fine buildings.

Can you identify similar examples in your area (e.g. Richill, Killough, Moneymore, Glynn)?

Rural planning and redevelopment

Houses grow old and become outdated. Farmers naturally want to replace their old houses with new ones. Other people also feel a desire to live in the country, even if they work in an urban area. The car makes this possible. Planners have to decide what general policy to adopt, bearing in mind certain factors:

- Random isolated building makes it expensive to provide services (water, sewerage, electricity, telephone, refuse disposal). It can, if carelessly done, spoil the beauty of the countryside. On the other hand, should freedom of choice be limited if the builder is prepared to pay for the extra costs involved?
- If rural housing is limited to replacement of old farmhouses, children of farmers as they grow up will have to leave the rural areas for the towns. They would leave behind an ageing population.
- The building of groups of new houses in the open countryside has been particularly criticised. Instead, the expansion of present villages where services are available already should be encouraged. Fewer children would then have to walk to school along roads without

Fig. 5.13. Cushendun village.

footpaths. Fewer additional access points on to main roads would be necessary.

Some of the true villages in the province are survivals from estate or 'demesne' villages, established adjacent to a landlord's mansion. The letting and the building of houses, often in a uniform style, was under his personal control. Everyone in the village worked on his estate. The school, church and social facilities were strongly influenced by the landlord as patron. Class distinctions were strictly observed.

We now build in a variety of styles. We try to give everyone equal freedom to work, build and travel as they wish. Should we discipline ourselves by planning to conserve old buildings and beautiful façades in our villages as in the towns (see fig. 5.13), and by requiring that new buildings fit in aesthetically with the old? When there is a demand for rural residences for urban workers, should we plan appropriate commuter villages in the same way that we have developed new towns to absorb overspill populations (see fig. 5.14)?

Exercises

1. (i) What does fig. 5.15 say about the value of houses over time? Is this always true? Give examples from Northern Ireland.
   (ii) Looking at fig. 5.15, what is the effect of improvement grants? What advantages does this policy have over complete clearance and rebuilding (which is usually cheaper overall)?
2. (a) Try to measure 'the beauty of the landscape'. Choose a strip of land on a 1:50,000 OS map (a length of coastline would be suitable). Then give each kilometre square a score:

   Habitat Give 1 mark each if any of the following are present:

tidal water	rough heathland
river	sand-dunes
lake	woodland
sand, shingle or mud beach	cliffs

Fig. 5.14. A design for a modern house. Does this kind of home fit comfortably into the Ulster rural landscape? Would it fit into Cushendun village (fig. 5.13)?

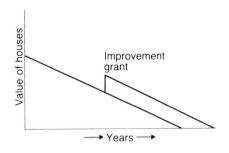

Fig. 5.15. The effects of time and improvement grants on house values.

Fig. 5.16. An area of Londonderry ready for redevelopment.

Relief Amplitude (i.e. difference between highest and lowest point):
    Over 150 metres   give 3 marks
    100–150 metres   give 2 marks
Nature Reserve   give 4 marks
Historical building   give 3 marks

Draw a sketch of the area and devise a scheme of shading the grid squares in five intensities from areas scoring over 8 marks to those scoring 1 or less.

(b) The basic assumption of this evaluation is 'The greater the variety, the higher the scenic and environmental quality'. Does the scheme reward the right qualities? Can you suggest improvements to the scheme?

3. Try your hand at the 'small steps' strategy of housing redevelopment. Fig. 5.16 is part of the Brandywell area, Londonderry, before redevelopment. There are approximately 200 house sites on the 2.5 hectares of land.
   (a) Plan to house 77 families after redevelopment.
   (b) Retain and modernise as many as possible of the 'fit' and the 'unfit but repairable' houses.
   (c) Preserve Brandywell Road as a throughway.
   (d) Re-draw the area as you would like it to become.
   (e) See if you can organise a phased building programme dealing with about 20 houses at a time. (There must at any time be accommodation in the area for 77 families, even if you have to supply mobile homes on empty sites for a time.)
   (f) When you have finished (and not before) turn to page 94 to see a professional planner's solution to the problem. Compare the two proposals.

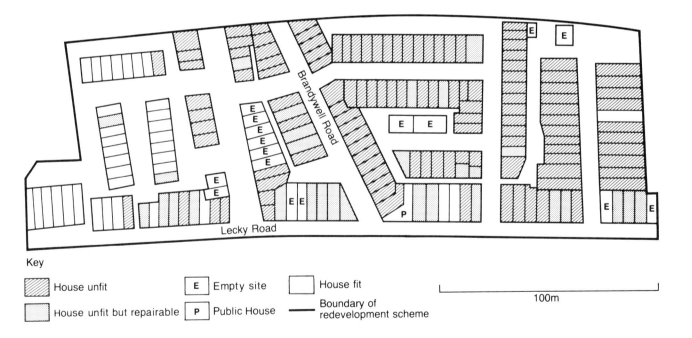

6 Patterns in the city

What is Belfast like and what is it like to live there? Here are two descriptions of Belfast, both written by 15-year-old pupils at schools in the city:

'Belfast isn't a very interesting place. There aren't many places to go. It has lots of bricked-up buildings and blank spaces where buildings have been bombed. It's often smoggy and damp. It's OK.' (Tricia Herd)

'Belfast has a varied skyline with domes, spires and modern office blocks. It has typical city shopping with Marks and Spencers in the middle. There are lots of pigeons.' (Paul Rea)

Which description fits your perception of the city best? One reason for such different images of the city is that the city is such a varied place. No one image can possibly describe the whole of *any* city. All cities are made up of very different areas, each with its own distinctive character and function. Belfast is no different.

Fig. 6.1. Land use zones in Belfast.

Key

- - - Belfast urban area stopline, the limit on urban development and sprawl imposed by planning regulations (drawn in 1963)

▨ CBD
1 Inner residential
2 Outer residential
■ Industrial
▨ Open space

Fig. 6.2. The population growth of Belfast.

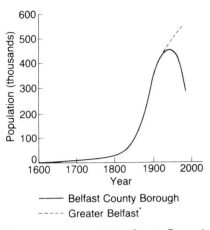

— Belfast County Borough
---- Greater Belfast*

*Greater Belfast = Belfast County Borough and boroughs of Castlereagh, North Down, Lisburn and Newtownabbey.

Fig. 6.3. Belfast city centre. This photograph was taken from the top floor of Windsor House overlooking Belfast's city centre. At 22 storeys high it is the tallest building in Ireland. Residential land is not common in the CBD, but the caretaker of Windsor House lives on the top floor of this building. Are there any advantages for him living in this part of the city? Are there any disadvantages?

As you can see on fig. 6.1, the built-up area of Belfast can be divided up into a number of such units. Around the city centre there is an area mainly composed of offices, department stores and specialist shops. This part of a city is usually known as the Central Business District (CBD). Outside the CBD there are different types of residential areas. These range from rows of compact terraced housing to areas where large detached houses set in their own grounds are the most common type of dwelling. In other parts the city landscape is dominated by the factories, warehouses and storage depots of industry. The CBD, residential areas and industrial zones all fit together like a huge jigsaw to form the built-up area of the city.

Which land use type shown on the map has not been mentioned so far? Is there any pattern to the distribution of open spaces for recreation in Belfast?

The city grows

The overall pattern of land use in Belfast is one which has grown and developed over a long period of time. In 1981 there were 595,000 people living in Greater Belfast; you can see from fig. 6.2 how the population has grown since the sixteenth century.

The city began as a small group of houses sited at a fording place over the River Lagan at the head of Belfast Lough. This became an important crossing point on a route which linked Counties Antrim and Down. By 1685 there was a population of 2,000 on the west bank of the Lagan. When the Long Bridge over the river was opened in 1688 the settlement began to spread to the east bank as well.

The fastest period of expansion came in the eighteenth century when factories began to be built in the town. Up to this time all production was based in people's homes since there was no power supply that could be harnessed for mass production. By the 1780s, however, the water-wheel had been invented and factories for spinning cotton began to be built in west Belfast near streams which flowed off the Antrim Plateau.

The town began to attract people from the surrounding rural areas who came to work in these factories. In 1830 the first steam-driven machinery was introduced and this began a new phase of expansion so that during the next century the town grew to become the most important manufacturing centre in Ireland. The story of linen and shipbuilding in the city, told in chapter 7, had much to do with this success.

The striking thing about the land use in the central part of the city is the dominance of certain types of shops. They are mostly large department stores or smaller shops which sell specialist items such as jewellery. The other common land uses here are the offices of local government departments and private businesses (fig. 6.3).

The reasons for these particular land uses being so common in the CBD have to do with competition for space. Department stores, chain stores and company offices are attracted to this area partly because of the prestige of having a city centre address. This is a popular area for these land uses and there is competition between them for the most accessible locations. Department and chain stores need a large number of customers to stay in business. This makes them keen to occupy a site which has roads coming from all parts of the city. Offices employ large numbers of people who need to be able to get to work and home again reasonably easily. Offices also tend to group together in one part of the

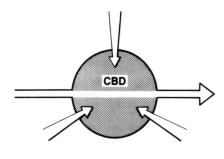

Fig. 6.4. Movement into the city.

Fig. 6.5. Traffic flow on the Lisburn Road over 24 hours. When do the major peak flows occur? What do you think causes them? When do the minor peak flows occur? What causes these minor peaks?

Fig. 6.6. Rush-hour traffic in Belfast. The people in this picture are having to put up with a long delay because of traffic congestion. They are also having to cope with noise from engines and fumes from exhausts. It would be very difficult, if not impossible, to measure the cost of these delays, but it must be very great. What are some of these costs?

city. This cuts down the time spent in sending information from one office block to another. A combination of these reasons leads to fierce competition for the best sites.

The land use which can afford to pay the highest price for a particular site usually gets it.

Movements in the city

About one in every four people who work in Belfast works in the central area of the city. If we include shoppers with the people travelling to work, the number of people coming into the city centre each weekday totals about 35,000. About 22,000 of these travel by car and the rest travel by bus or train. There are also those people who travel across the city and only pass through this central area. These different kinds of journey are shown in fig. 6.4.

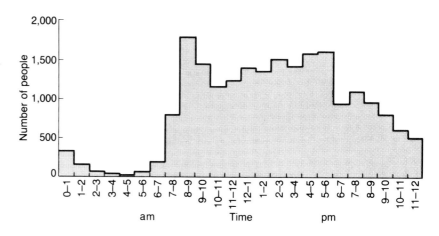

If all these journeys were evenly spread over time there would be few traffic problems in the city centre. However, fig. 6.5 shows that the amount of traffic on a typical road leading to the city centre varies greatly through the day.

Figure 6.6 was taken near Belfast's city centre during the morning peak traffic period. One major problem produced by traffic congestion in the CBD is a reduction in the number of shoppers coming to the area. When few people owned cars the fact that all bus routes in Belfast converged on the city centre gave shops in the CBD a big advantage: most people had to use the buses to do their shopping and so most people used city centre shops. However, a staggering increase in car ownership over the years (fig. 6.7) has increased traffic congestion in peak hours and even made it difficult for shoppers to find a convenient place to park. Increased car ownership has given people a greater choice of where to shop because they can travel further in the same time and go in almost any direction, not just along bus routes. As a result suburban locations have become just as accessible to large numbers of shoppers as the CBD has been up to now. The CBD is fast losing its one big advantage: accessibility. At the same time owners of shops and businesses in the CBD are finding that locations in other parts of the city and even beyond the city limits altogether, have other advantages:

(a) The annual rates bill paid to the City Council for services such as rubbish collection is much lower.

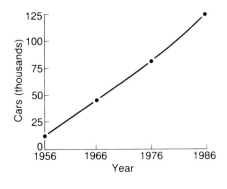

Fig. 6.7. Car ownership in Belfast, 1956–86.

Fig. 6.8. The distribution of engineering firms in Belfast: (a) 1959 (b) 1979.

(b) If the business is successful there will be more room for expansion later.
(c) It is much cheaper to buy land outside the CBD.
(d) Car parking can be provided on site, making it easier for shoppers to take away the goods they have bought. This is becoming more of an advantage with the growing trend of buying food in bulk for storage in home freezers.

As a result many new shops and businesses are sited at accessible points outside the CBD and some others have decided to move out to these locations from old premises near the city centre (fig. 6.8). There are many ways in which the problem of city centre congestion can be reduced:

- One-way road systems and off-street car parking help by increasing the amount of road space available for moving traffic.
- An increase in flexi-time working would help to spread the volume of traffic in the streets during rush-hours over a longer period.
- A third possibility might be to encourage more people to use public transport.

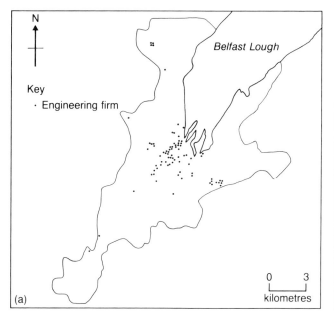

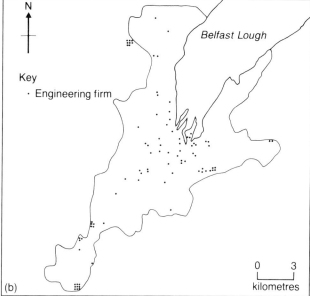

Fig. 6.9. A comparison of road space used and passengers carried in public and private transport.

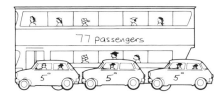

Figure 6.9 shows that a bus can carry 77 passengers. About three cars will fit in the same road space used by one bus. These cars could carry a maximum of 15 people. So if people used buses to travel into the city centre rather than cars, much less road space would be needed. There would be less congestion on the roads.

Another way of tackling the problem is to divert some of the traffic not destined for the city centre on to new roads going around this area. This is the most expensive solution. In the 1960s planning consultants drew up elaborate plans for ring roads and urban motorways circling Belfast. These early plans are summarised in fig. 6.10. Very little of this scheme has been put into practice because by the early 1970s a number of things had happened:

- Attitudes to urban motorways had changed.
- There was less money available for elaborate schemes.
- The 'troubles' had made it difficult to get building started in some parts of the city.

Fig. 6.10. Main proposals of Transport Plan for Belfast 1969.

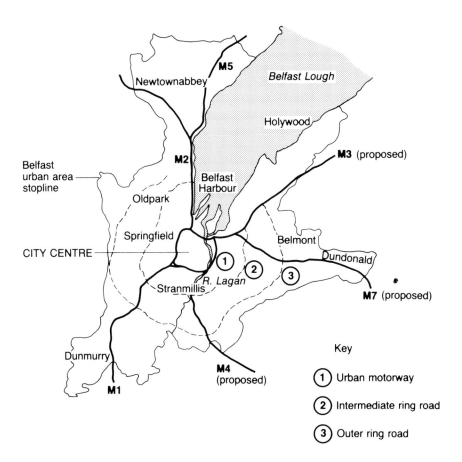

- The population of Belfast was now expected to decline rather than increase in the future.

After a public enquiry the government chose the strategy to be followed. There decision is summarised on fig. 6.12, but even this plan has not been strictly adhered to.

Fig. 6.11. 'Good morning, I'm from the Council. I've come to advise you of the proposed urban motorway route.'

Fig. 6.12. The proposed road extensions planned in the Government's 1978 city transport strategy.

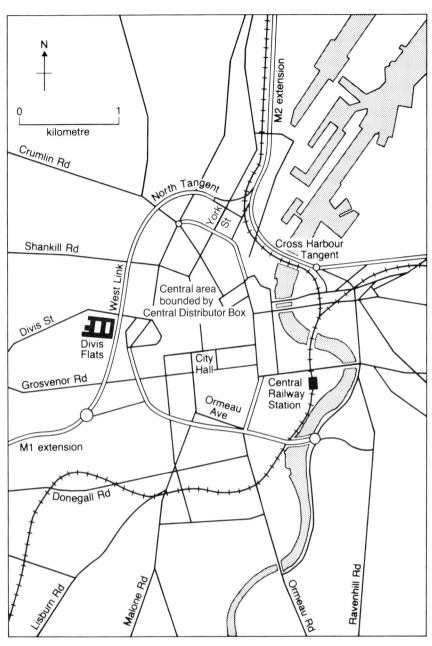

Original scheme   **1978 decision**

① Urban motorway

    Phase 1   Reduce urban motorway to dual carriageway linking M1 and M2 – known as the West Link

    Phase 2   Only to be built if the West Link does not result in reduced traffic flow over the Lagan bridges. It *may* also include a railway bridge

    Phase 3   Scrapped

② Intermediate ring road   Scrapped

③ Outer ring road   Mostly built by 1978

Living in the city

The inner residential area

Fig. 6.13. An inner residential area: Joy Street.

The office blocks, department stores and cinemas of the CBD are surrounded by the inner residential area. Joy Street (fig. 6.13) is part of this area. The houses nearest the camera are town houses built in the eighteenth century when some of the wealthy merchants of Belfast had their 'genteel residences' here. At the far end of the street, and further from the CBD, are much smaller terraced houses. Tens of thousands of these were built in the city as the population grew from about 50,000 in 1830 to 350,000 by 1900. Today most of the buildings in this area are coming to the end of their useful life. Joy Street is now part of the Cromac Redevelopment Area in which about 560 new and renovated houses, a primary school, sites for light industry, a community and day centre and shops are being built.

The outer residential area

Fig. 6.14. An outer residential area: Castlereagh.

Between 1900 and 1950 there were many improvements in the public and private transport system which meant that people did not have to live so close to their place of work. As a result, beyond the terraced housing of the inner residential area another residential area grew up, mainly along the major road and railway routes. This outer residential area has houses built both by private builders and by the City Council which conformed to much stricter building regulations on quality and density (fig. 6.14). The result has been that the most common land use in this area is semi-detached and detached housing. More attention was also paid to the general layout of the area: cul-de-sac and crescent-shaped streets were introduced to provide a more varied road pattern, and grassy areas landscaped with trees, along with gardens to each house, have helped to give this area an open and attractive appearance.

The suburbs

Fig. 6.15. The suburbs: public housing on the Poleglass estate.

The enormous increase in car ownership in Belfast during the last thirty years (from 12,500 in 1956 to 125,000 in 1986) means that people can now live much further from the city centre and still be within reach of their work. Many people are prepared to make this daily journey to work because they like living in a suburb. Here they have access to open countryside *and* to the shops, schools, clubs and other services of the city!

But there was another factor leading to the growth of suburbs: the city's growing population combined with people displaced as a result of slum clearance in the inner residential area led to a demand for thousands of new homes. The only area with enough space for these new housing 'estates' was the open land on the edge of the city. The demand for houses made suburbs necessary and the increase in car ownership made them possible.

Public housing areas in the suburbs such as the Poleglass estate have a variety of house types (fig. 6.15). They range from two-bedroomed bungalows for old people to high-rise flats. Amenities such as shops for everyday items, schools, churches and community halls are part of their layout. Privately-built suburbs such as Upper Malone tend to be rather different: here there are mostly large detached houses or bungalows set in spacious gardens. Amenities are not usually included in the plan for these areas. Private developers don't see this as their responsibility. Such suburban areas, almost completely lacking in amenities, have been called 'housing deserts'.

Residential segregation

From what you have read so far you may not think that Belfast is any different from many other European cities. Like them it has a CBD. It also has industrial, residential and recreational areas. It suffers like most cities from traffic congestion, pollution and the need to replace old, decayed buildings.

Fig. 6.16. The 'peace line' in Belfast, built by the Army between Protestant/Unionist and Catholic/Nationalist areas in west Belfast. The aim was to increase security and reduce tension between the two communities.

Yet Belfast makes the news more regularly than most British cities. Much of what is reported has to do with 'the troubles' (fig. 6.16). The people of Northern Ireland are not only divided by class and culture; they are also torn apart by religious and political loyalties. These subdivisions are reflected in Belfast. Most residential areas in the city, especially the low-status areas of west Belfast, are segregated along religious lines. There are Roman Catholic/Nationalist areas and Protestant/Unionist areas. The boundaries between these areas are very sharp. In some places the boundary is a factory site, or a railway track. In others the boundary is only the width of a street.

One geographer made a study of two adjacent residential areas in west Belfast just before the present 'troubles' began. They are marked on fig. 6.17. The two study areas were Clonard and part of the Shankill. As Table 7 shows, both areas were quite similar in terms of class and status. The striking difference was that Clonard's population was 98% Catholic while the Shankill area was 99% Protestant.

Table 7 *A comparison of Shankill and Clonard.*

Residential area	Type of housing	Size of household	% of households with no car	Religion (% RC)
Shankill	Victorian terrace	3.3	85	1
Clonard	Victorian terrace	3.9	71	98

The distribution of the 271 homes responding to the questionnaire is shown on fig. 6.18. It shows that the inner parts of both Clonard and the Shankill were completely segregated by religion. The only parts where mixing occurred were along streets forming the boundaries of the two areas. Since 1969 when the 'peace line' was built between these two communities, the level of segregation is likely, if anything, to have increased.

The survey also found that people had a high concentration of activity within their own religious 'territory'. In a sample week it was found that 79% of all visits made by people living in the Shankill were made to other Protestant areas in the city. Only 4% of visits were to Catholic

Fig. 6.17. The distribution of religions in Belfast.

Key
- - - City boundary
Mainly Protestant
Mainly Catholic
'Peace line'

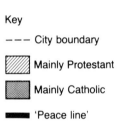

Fig. 6.18. Religious distribution in a small area of west Belfast. This map represents a sample of 10% of the people over the age of 21 in the two areas.

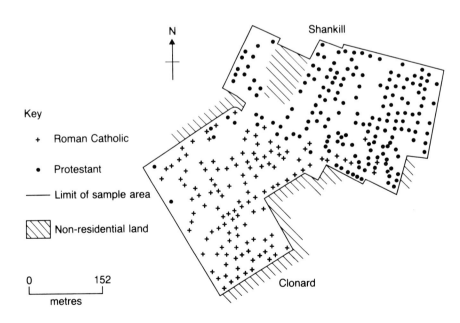

Key
+ Roman Catholic
• Protestant
— Limit of sample area
Non-residential land

areas. As Table 8 shows, the residents of Clonard showed a similar pattern of activity: the vast majority of their visits were made within Catholic areas of the city.

Table 8 *Visits made by residents of the Shankill and Clonard areas.*

Residential area	Visits in the city per week	
	% within Protestant areas	% within Catholic areas
Shankill	79	4
Clonard	5	88

The different 'orientation' of the Protestant and Roman Catholic areas was also interesting. Table 9 shows that support for Glasgow Celtic Football Club was very strong in Catholic Clonard. It was non-existent in the Protestant Shankill. Similar scores were found with newspaper readership: the *Irish News* had a large number of readers in Clonard but very few in the Shankill area. The two cultural and news media held in common were television and the *Belfast Telegraph* evening paper, but there was little else.

Table 9 *'Orientation' of residents of the Shankill and Clonard areas.*

Residential area	% reading *Irish News*	% supporting Glasgow Celtic	% reading *Belfast Telegraph*	% with TV sets
Shankill	13	0	68	86
Clonard	83	73	58	77

Craigavon New Town

Following the report by Sir Robert Matthew in 1963 on the Belfast Urban Area, an exciting plan for the development of a completely New Town in Northern Ireland was produced. The aims of building this **New Town**, which the government named Craigavon, were
- to provide a pleasant residential area which would be an alternative to Belfast, so easing housing and traffic problems in the city
- to provide an attractive location for new industries
- to provide a centre which would bring new life to the southern and western parts of the province.

Make a list of the things you think would be necessary for these aims to be achieved.

One major problem facing the planners of Craigavon was the lack of identity which inhabitants of New Towns often experience. This feeling that 'it's going to be a great town one day but at the moment it's Endsville because there's nothing to do' is almost inevitable in a New Town. No matter how well it has been planned it is just not possible to produce an instant town with established activities and

New Towns
Towns built in rural areas to relieve congestion in the large cities and provide a pleasant living and working environment for their new inhabitants.

institutions. One reason for selecting the site between Lurgan and Portadown was that these existing towns would help to reduce this problem (fig. 6.19). They would provide the social and recreational activities which the newcomers to Craigavon could take advantage of while they were being developed in their own area.

Fig. 6.19. The location of Craigavon New Town.

Two residential sectors, named Brownlow and Mandeville, form the central section of the New Town (fig. 6.20). The plan for these sectors had the following aims:
- Provision of a varied range of houses in separate clusters of between 50 and 200 dwellings.
- Spacious house planning, together with good car parking and garaging.
- The provision of local services in the heart of the neighbourhood units which make up each sector to provide day-to-day needs within easy walking distance of all homes. Services provided at Moyraverty centre in Brownlow, for example, include 1 supermarket, 6 shops, a community hall, a pub, offices, 2 churches and a primary school.
- The grouping of secondary schools to form a central recreation and education campus for the use of the whole community.
- The separation of main pedestrian and cycle tracks from the roads and the construction of house clusters around culs-de-sac to keep through traffic out of residential areas.

The city centre of Craigavon is situated immediately to the north of Brownlow and Mandeville sectors. It includes the town hall and a full range of high-order offices and shops. To the south-west are grouped the sports centre, area hospital and technical college, whilst to the east is the city park and lake. Industrial districts are located outside residential areas mainly to the north of the city beside the M1 motorway and the Belfast to Dublin railway (fig. 6.21).

Look back at the lists of things you considered necessary for a successful town. To what extent have these been planned for in Craigavon?

Fig. 6.20. Craigavon New Town.

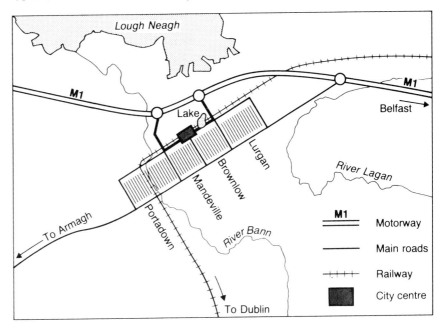

Despite a carefully prepared plan for the city, Craigavon has been affected by a number of unfortunate developments. The building programme began in the 'boom' period of the 1960s when there seemed to be no shortage of money for large projects of this kind. This period was followed, however, by the stringent seventies when economic cutbacks were the order of the day. This had two effects on Craigavon: (a) there was less money spent by the government on the New Town than had been earmarked for it in the original plan, and therefore fewer services were provided; (b) the economic recession led to less industrial growth than had been originally expected. This produced a decline in the demand for new industrial sites and made it difficult to attract enough firms to the city.

A second problem was that Craigavon had to compete with other expanding towns such as Bangor and Newtownards which proved more attractive to many migrants. These towns were still within easy commuting distance of Belfast.

The third problem which arose proved to be the most difficult to deal with: rumours spread about the problems of children having to change schools, about a lack of shopping facilities, the difficulty strangers found in making new friends, and the vandalising of empty houses. As a result of these rumours the town developed a poor image. Despite government incentives in the form of mobility grants totalling £450 per household and massive publicity campaigns, the population increase did not keep up with the original targets. Today Craigavon is slowly finding its feet as a viable community.

Exercises

1. Conduct a survey which compares your class's image of Belfast with that of other cities in the British Isles.

Fig. 6.21. Housing and walkways in Craigavon.

2. Why has the population in Belfast County Borough been declining since 1971 while the overall population of Greater Belfast continues to rise?
3. What economic or environmental arguments could have been used against the plan for an urban motorway in Belfast? Write a short report to the public enquiry giving your views.
4. An interesting way of comparing the standard of amenities in different residential areas is to work out an 'amenity index' for each. Take at least two residences in your local area which are far enough apart not to use all the same amenities. For each amenity pace out or use a map to measure the distance from the house to the nearest place where it is provided. Give amenities which are not provided within walking distance an agreed high number, say 3,000. Add all the distances together and divide by the number of amenities to calculate the average.

You could set it out like this:

Address ....

Amenity	Number of paces from house
1 Bus stop	200
2 Railway station	3,000 (beyond walking distance)
3 Primary school	620
4 Grocer	804
5 Butcher	793
6 Newsagent	416
7 Chemist	876
8 Playing field or park	1,765
9 Telephone box (working!)	39
10 Library	942
Add up to total	9,455

Divide by 10 (the total number of amenities) to calculate the Amenity Index = *945.5*.

A low index means that an area is well supplied with amenities while a high index suggests poor facilities in a 'housing desert'.

5. (a) What are the factors which either encourage or force people to live in religiously segregated areas in Belfast?
   (b) What other types of residential segregation exist in British cities?

7 Establishing industries

If you were going to set up a business which manufactured something, what would you need to get you started? You would need somewhere to do your work – perhaps a garage converted into a workshop or a larger factory building. You would need machinery and a power supply to operate it and provide light and heat. You would need the raw materials or components out of which you would manufacture your product and some means of transporting them to your workshop. You might also want to employ other people in your firm which would mean finding the sort of people who have the skills you need (unless you are going to train them). All this would be quite impossible, however, without money to pay for it. This money is known as 'capital'. It usually has to be borrowed and then paid back in small amounts with interest over a long period.

Fig. 7.1. A flow diagram of costs in industry.

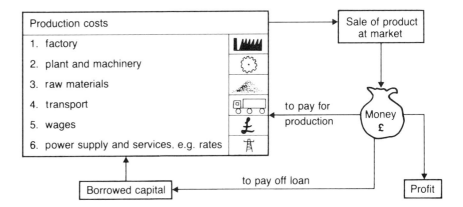

As you can see in fig. 7.1, borrowed capital will get you started in production. But to stay in production, you will need profits from the sale of your product. Success in the long term depends on having a product which people want to buy and making sure that proceeds from this sale are greater than the cost of production.

An added problem is that once the decision to start manufacturing has been taken, circumstances can change. These changes force managers to make new decisions about how to adjust their businesses so that they will keep making profits and remain successful. In this chapter we will look at why some industries have been set up in Northern Ireland and what decisions have been taken in adjusting to changes over time.

The linen industry

The raw material for linen cloth is flax, a crop which is particularly suited to the moist climate and types of soil found in Ireland. In the early eighteenth century when linen was becoming an established industry in

Fig. 7.2. The stages of linen production.

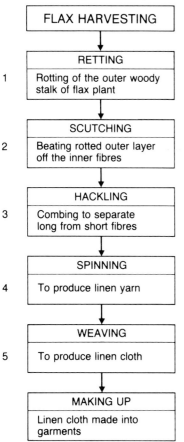

Northern Ireland, the large number of rivers and streams was another asset: in those days water power was used to drive machinery.

The settling in the province of Huguenot and Scottish businessmen who knew the best methods of flax culture was also important (fig. 7.2). They knew the kinds of cloth most in demand in other countries, and many of them were already rich and able to invest capital in the industry (fig. 7.3).

Linen production was a cottage industry until the 1820s when big changes came. In 1828 Thomas and Andrew Mulholland rebuilt their burnt-out cotton mill in Belfast as a flax-spinning mill. It proved to be very profitable. Their success encouraged others and the flax-spinning industry grew rapidly. This increased the supply of linen yarn, encouraging others to start weaving factories equipped with the newly invented power looms. These machines were introduced from about 1850 and the number of employees in the linen industry trebled within twenty-five years.

Better spinning and weaving machinery would have been pointless, however, if these changes had not been matched by some improvement in the method of transporting linen to market; otherwise the increased production could not have been sold. In 1824 the first regular service by cargo steamer was established between Belfast and Liverpool. This provided a quick, cheap and reliable means of transport to the English markets. Improvements to Belfast harbour also helped: in 1839 the docks and quays were extended, and a straight channel was cut out to deep water in the lough so that large ships could be docked. Before this, large ships had to anchor offshore and load cargo into their holds from barges.

Greater trade through the ports and the increased use of imported coal for steam-driven machinery benefited Belfast more than any other

Fig. 7.3. Brown linen markets, 1816.

net output
The value of materials produced minus the costs involved in their production.

Fig. 7.4. An old advertisement for Irish linen.

Fig. 7.5. Fashion garments made from linen.

part of the country. Production costs were lower in this area. By about 1850 more than 30% of all the linen mills in Ireland were in or near Belfast and many of the linen markets in country areas were beginning to close down.

For a great many years – until the 1950s – flax growing and the production of linen continued as major parts of Northern Ireland's agricultural and industrial scene. In 1949 the linen industry employed over 58,000 people and was producing 28.6% of **net output** (fig 7.4 and Table 10). As the figures show, however, the industry has been in deep trouble since this period.

Table 10 *Employment and net output in the linen industry, 1949–78.*

	1949	1958	1968	1978
Employees	58,300	43,100	25,200	13,000
Net output*	28.6	14	7	5.4

* As a percentage of total net output of all industries in Northern Ireland.

There are two main reasons for this decline:
1. competition from other countries; and
2. competition from other products.
1. After the Second World War, some countries deliberately restricted their imports of linen because they wanted to allow their own textile industries to expand. This meant that some countries, notably Brazil, which had previously been good markets for Irish linen, became producers and began competing with Irish firms for sales.
2. Competition also grew from linen's most important natural rival, cotton. The British cotton industry had to cope with imports of cheap cotton from abroad but it was a much larger industry than the linen industry. It was able to reorganise quickly with the result that even British-produced cotton was much cheaper than linen. In addition there was competition from man-made fibres such as nylon and polyester. The improved technology and mass production techniques used in their production made them cheaper than flax yarns. When woven into fabrics their greater crease-resistance also gave them the edge in the competitive world of fashion. Linen producers were slow to respond to this competition and the man-made fabric producers have been able to establish their products as everyday items in our wardrobes and 'linen' cupboards.

Today many firms have gone out of business but others have grouped together so that the industry still survives.

Attempts are being made to re-establish flax as a local crop. Northern Ireland imports over £8 million worth of flax every year so any that can be produced locally will help. Research carried out recently at the Lambeg Industrial Research Institute (LIRA) near Lisburn, has shown that the retting process can be simplified by spraying the crop with special herbicides. If field experiments are successful this might encourage local farmers to begin growing flax as a commercial crop once again.

There are other signs that linen is beginning to make a comeback: in the fashion trade there has been an increase in demand for natural fibres (fig. 7.5), and the emphasis is on leisure wear. Fashions change, but people will probably have even more leisure time in the future.

If the Irish linen industry can develop easy-care linen mixtures it might be able to exploit this growing market and enter a period of expansion once again.

The Herdman Mill

One of the first flax spinning mills in Ireland was started by the Herdman family in 1835 on the banks of the River Mourne, near Strabane (figs. 7.6 and 7.7). The mill was built on this particular site for two main reasons: the ready supply of water from the river needed in the manufacturing process and for generating power; and the fact that the Duke of Abercorn encouraged the Herdman family by leasing them land which was part of his estate.

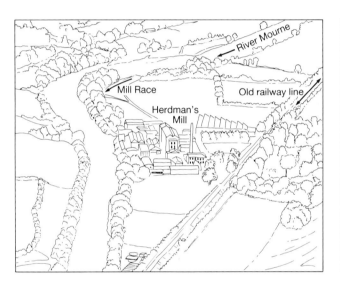

Fig. 7.6. An aerial view of the Herdman Mill.

The company started with only 75 people, mostly women, but the workforce had expanded to nearly 700 people by 1845. To house their employees the company built the village of Sion Mills close to the factory – about 200 small yellow-washed cottages of local stone. As you can see from fig. 7.8, employment in the mill rose to a peak of 1,200 in 1951 but has declined to about 650 today.

For the first hundred years the mill used only locally-grown flax. From the 1930s, when flax-growing began to decline in Ulster, the company turned to raw material from abroad. The mill today uses 50 tonnes of flax per week. It is grown in Normandy in northern France, scutched and retted in Belgium and transported to Sion Mills in containers by road and sea ferry. Most flax is imported through Belfast harbour, but Warrenpoint has been used occasionally.

Production of pure linen yarn has declined to about 75% of what it was in the late 1950s. A quarter of the company's total production is now of linen and man-made fibre mixtures. So while the linen industry in general has been declining, Herdman's have managed to maintain their overall level of production quite well. This has been achieved by
- investing in modern spinning machinery which needs less labour
- searching for new markets and being willing to adapt the product

Fig. 7.7. The location of Sion Mills.

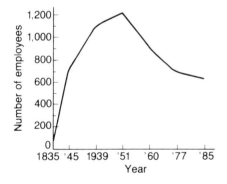

Fig. 7.8. Employees in the Herdman Mill, 1835–1985.

when customers demand a certain type of yarn or want it packaged in a different way for their specific needs.

Only 8% of the mill's production is sold for the home market, going to Northern Ireland weaving firms. About 40% of what is exported goes to one country – Italy – and the rest is sold to other countries including Japan, Australia and the United States.

The shipbuilding industry

Belfast has become world-famous for its link with shipbuilding. Edward Harland bought a shipyard there in 1858. Under his management the firm expanded quickly and in 1861 he took on a partner, Gustav Wolff, to help him run the business.

The Harland and Wolff partnership brought many new ideas to ship construction. They increased the length of their ships without making them wider; this gave more carrying capacity with no decrease in speed. They put on steel rather than wooden upper decks so that their ships were constructed like box-girders; this made them very strong. Willingness to experiment and adopt new design ideas helped to put Harland and Wolff ahead of their competitors and kept the yard busy with new orders. In the period up to the First World War many famous liners were built: notably the *Oceanic*, and her sister ship the *Titanic*.

During both World Wars the yard was used to construct and repair a large number of naval vessels. Despite attacks by German bombers in 1941 which destroyed about 60% of the company's production capacity, Harland and Wolff built 6 aircraft carriers, 2 cruisers, 2 large depot ships,

47 corvettes, 29 minesweepers, 9 frigates and 44 other vessels.

The wartime bombing had one benefit: it left the yard with modern equipment once the rebuilding had been completed. For a time after 1945 the yard did very well. There was plenty of work to be done refitting ships for peacetime and replacing those which had been sunk. At that time 30,000 men were employed.

But there were troubled times ahead: the first indication of those troubles came in 1958. In that year the number of passengers crossing the Atlantic by air was, for the first time, greater than those travelling by sea. This was a sign that the market for passenger liners on which Harland and Wolff's growth had depended was beginning to fade away.

At the same time, Japanese and other foreign shipyards began to compete very strongly for new orders. These two factors – a declining market and increasing competition – forced the company to make some big changes. They decided to go for an ambitious plan. It involved changing the yard's speciality from building ocean liners to building supertankers.

Huge amounts of money provided by the government were spent on re-equipping the yard. Here was the world's largest building dock, capable of producing a million-tonne ship. It was straddled by two giant cranes, Goliath and Samson, which have become new landmarks for the city (fig. 7.9).

Going into the 1970s Harland and Wolff was among the best, competing strongly for new supertanker orders. Then the bottom fell out of the tanker market. Rocketing oil prices followed by a world recession resulted in millions of tonnes of shipping being tied up. Massive losses led to the yard being taken over by the government in 1974 to save jobs.

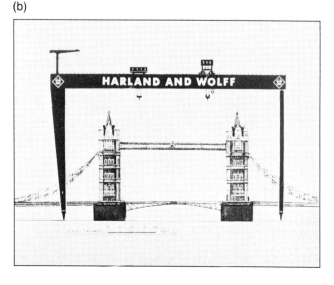

Fig. 7.9. Harland and Wolff's building dock: (a) an aerial view; (b) a drawing of one of the huge overhead cranes with London's Tower Bridge drawn to the same scale.

Fig. 7.10. SWOPS. This is the first ship of its kind in the world. It is an oil tanker with a flexible pipeline which can be lowered 200 metres from the ship to the seabed. The pipeline is attached to an oilwell with the help of a small submarine. Computers keep the ship in place in up to Force 9 gales while the oil is being pumped out. The oil can be processed and stored in the ship before it is delivered to market.

As the slump continued into the late 1970s, the company struggled to survive. It had to make do with snapping up what it could in the building of smaller cargo and ferry boats. The workforce fell from 12,000 in 1969 to 8,500 in 1979. In a bid to find work the company opened its new engine-building yard to general engineering contracts. Orders for heavy steel equipment were obtained, including the structure of the new Foyle Bridge in Londonderry. Diversification became the name of the game.

The market for ships remains depressed in the 1980s. Harland and Wolff's workforce has been further trimmed to 5,500, but the company has kept fighting for orders. The old willingness to experiment landed them an important contract from BP in 1984. It was for a Single Well Oil Production System, nicknamed SWOPS (fig. 7.10).

So shipbuilding in Belfast is surviving. Harland and Wolff believe that their reinvestment and re-equipment programme will make them competitive with any yard in the world when the demand for ships returns.

Decisions for the present

One of the most difficult problems facing Northern Ireland since the Second World War has been a shortage of jobs. This has happened because of two things which combine to affect the supply and demand for labour. Firstly, Northern Ireland has had a higher than average crude birth rate. In 1981 there were 176 live births per 1,000 population (compared with 128 per 1,000 in the United Kingdom as a whole). This has led to a big increase in the population of working age – the *supply* of labour.

Secondly, the decline in the province's traditional industries has produced a decline in the *demand* for labour. Almost 80,000 jobs were lost in the shipbuilding, textiles and clothing industries between 1950 and 1980. That is a decline of just over 60%! In 1950 these three sectors made up two-thirds of manufacturing employment in Northern Ireland: by 1980 this had fallen to 40%.

primary employment sector
Industries producing the basic raw materials, such as timber and fuels, which can then be used by other industries.

secondary employment sector
Industries which use the raw materials and the fuels produced by the primary sector to make or manufacture various goods.

tertiary employment sector
Does not make anything, but provides the transport and other services which people need to work and live.

As labour supply has increased and the demand for labour has decreased the problem of unemployment has grown.

Employment structures

The government is also concerned about the employment structure in Northern Ireland. Manufacturing industries, such as engineering, are only one of the three main sectors into which industries can be divided. The other two sectors are the **primary and tertiary sectors**.

Table 11 *Employment in Northern Ireland by industrial sectors, 1960–80.*

	1960		1970		1982	
	No. of jobs (thousands)	%	No. of jobs (thousands)	%	No. of jobs (thousands)	%
Primary	22.5	5.0	15.8	3.25	10.8	2.3
Secondary	218.0	48.5	223.3	45.9	132.8	28.0
Tertiary	208.8	46.5	247.2	50.85	329.9	69.7
Total	449.3	100	486.3	100	473.5	100

The majority of people employed in the tertiary sector are not producing anything to sell and are not therefore making much money for the community. Yet this is the sector which has been expanding *most*. As the employment figures in Table 11 show, between 1960 and 1982 tertiary sector jobs in Northern Ireland rose from 46% to over 69% of the total.

The government's role

Faced with these problems, what would you do? Obviously more manufacturing jobs are needed. Let us look at the factors working against expansion in this sector:
- A small market
- High transport costs
- Expensive power supplies
- Political unrest.

Northern Ireland has a population of about 1½ million. That is about the same as East Anglia. If you can imagine a moat of 30 kilometres wide around East Anglia's border it will give you some idea of Northern Ireland's problems!

A small market of 1½ million means that many firms have to sell their products outside the region. This makes it difficult to keep in touch with customers and their needs. It also makes it more difficult to stay competitive, because Northern Irish firms have to pay higher transport costs: raw materials often have to be imported, and the finished product has to be sold at a price which will cover that cost *and* the cost of transporting the product to market.

Northern Ireland has no coalfields (see chapter 2). Nor is it connected to the North Sea Gas distribution network. This lack of power resources means that oil and coal have to be imported for electricity generation, making the cost per unit of electricity higher than in most other parts of the United Kingdom (see Table 12). The mainland's National Grid does not extend across the Irish Sea and even the benefits of a link with Eire's electricity grid have been lost since the cross-border connection was blown up by the IRA in 1975.

Table 12 *Average price per kWh for large industrial electricity usage, 1984/85.*

Electricity board	Major city or town	Average price (p)
England and Wales		
South Western	Bristol	3.595
South Wales	Cardiff	3.556
London	London	3.489
Southern	Reading	3.488
Midlands	Wolverhampton	3.474
Yorkshire	Leeds	3.471
Merseyside & North Wales	Liverpool	3.453
North Eastern	Newcastle upon Tyne	3.437
East Midlands	Nottingham	3.427
South Eastern	Maidstone	3.400
North Western	Manchester	3.380
Eastern	Luton	3.350
Scotland		
South of Scotland	Glasgow	3.259
North of Scotland	Perth	3.182
Northern Ireland		
Northern Ireland Electricity Service	Belfast	3.595

'The troubles' in Northern Ireland have been another important factor in the bid to expand jobs. They affect the 'image' of the province as seen by businessmen from abroad.

On the other hand there are some factors which favour industrial expansion. Some of these are as follows:
- Lower wages for industrial workers than in all other regions
- A pool of skilled industrial workers
- Good industrial relations (few strikes)
- A good communications network
- Good schools and colleges

Look again at the flow diagram of costs in a factory (fig. 7.1 on page 67). Industrialists in Northern Ireland have higher than average costs in three of the six areas of production: raw materials, transport and power supplies.

What the government has tried to do is provide incentives for new manufacturing industries to come to the province and for existing industries to expand. These incentives have been aimed at relieving the area's high production costs. The government has used a number of tactics:
- Grants or loans
- Providing factories
- Fuel subsidies
- Employment subsidies
- Business advice

- Retraining schemes
- Improving communications
- Creation of enterprise zones

With what success? Well, these schemes began to operate from about 1945. By 1960 they produced 34,000 jobs in manufacturing industry. That was nearly 19% of total manufacturing jobs. In the following years the number rose sharply, reaching 66,700 by 1970 – almost 38% of the total. By 1980 the number had fallen slightly – to 57,676 jobs – but this was a time of recession for the national economy generally.

Over the period 1945 to 1975, 325 new projects were set up with the help from the government. Fig. 7.11 describes the trends over this time. There were two peaks; one immediately after the Second World War, and the other in the 1960s. However, since the 1970s there has been a general decline in the number of new openings.

This general decline, combined with an overall closure rate of 43% for the period 1945–79, gave cause for concern. The average lifespan of these government-assisted projects was only seven years. This would seem to be very poor value for money when each job started was costing over £17,000.

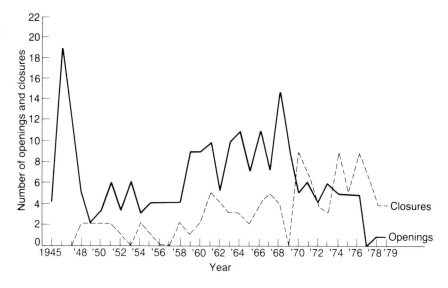

Fig. 7.11. Openings and closures of government-assisted, externally-owned manufacturing projects in Northern Ireland.

Distribution of projects

Another controversial aspect of government industrial policy results from the distribution of projects attracted to the province. Two-thirds of these firms went to locations within 45 kilometres of Belfast (see fig. 7.12). This clustering can be compared with three other patterns (shown in figs. 7.13, 7.14 and 7.15).

(a) The economic pattern: unemployment rates are lower and average incomes higher in the Belfast area than in the rest of the province.
(b) The religious pattern: Protestants are found predominantly in the east, Roman Catholics in the north, west and south.
(c) The political pattern: due to the rigid sectarian basis of politics in Northern Ireland, the political pattern is similar to the religious pattern. Up to 1972 when 'Direct Rule' was introduced, the minority Catholic community elected the Opposition to Northern Ireland's regional parliament at Stormont. Their MPs came from the

Fig. 7.12. The distribution of new industries in Northern Ireland, 1950–73.

peripheral parts of the province. Unionist MPs formed the government administration, elected mainly by the Protestant vote from the wealthier eastern counties.

The controversy is about what sort of correlation exists between these three patterns and the distribution of government-assisted industry.

Fig. 7.13. Unemployed males as a percentage of economically-active males in Northern Ireland, 1971.

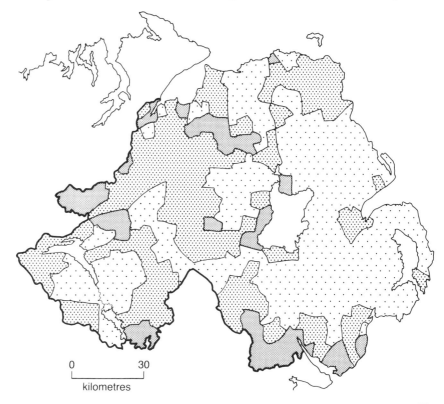

Fig. 7.14. Religious distribution in Northern Ireland.

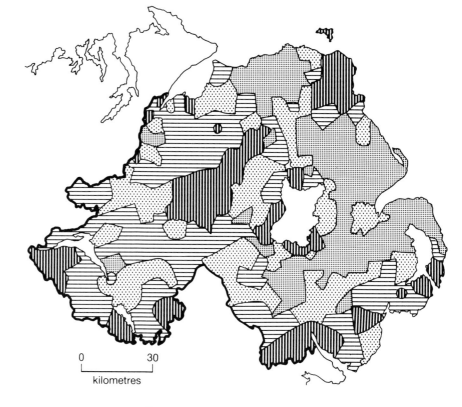

Key

- Over 75% Roman Catholic
- 45–75% Roman Catholic
- 45–75% Protestant
- Over 75% Protestant

Fig. 7.15. Voting patterns in Northern Ireland, 1922–72.

Key

- Always Official Unionist
- Always Nationalist

What links might there be?

Unionists claim that economic factors were the most important in producing the concentration of new industry in the east. When, for example, the tyre firm Michelin chose a location in Protestant Ballymena, the Unionist MP for North Antrim said,

'I believe that in his heart the Minister would rather the Michelin factory had gone either to Derry or near it. But he cannot say to it, "You must go there". If he does it goes to Scotland or the North East. We simply must be realistic about this.' (24 October 1967)

On the other hand Nationalists claim that political motives did operate. The MP for South Armagh could claim in Stormont that:

'We on this [Opposition] side of the House have done everything possible to get factories established in the Nationalist areas, but up to now we have been debarred by the bigotry and the narrow-mindedness of this government.' (15 December 1965).

Who is right? It is probably true to say that both sides can claim evidence which supports their point of view. Nationalists can call on the results of independent reports which reveal evidence of anti-Catholic discrimination in Ulster society. Unionists can equally point to studies of industrial development in other regions. These reports show that, despite the offer of big incentives, governments have little power to make firms go where they do not want to go.

Fig. 7.16. The location of Maydown Industrial Estate.

Case study: Maydown Industrial Estate

Maydown Industrial Estate is on the outskirts of Londonderry. There are ten factories here (fig. 7.16). The largest employer in Maydown is Peter England Ltd, manufacturing shirts and pyjamas. They have a workforce of 35 men and 320 women. The other firms located here are: Snare and Clayton Ltd, also making shirts; National Supply Co. (UK) Ltd, producing well-control systems for the oil industry; Hivolt Capacitors Ltd, making high-voltage capacitors; and Maydown Precision Engineering Ltd, manufacturing spare parts for cigarette machines. Between them these four firms employ 250 people, making a total of about 600 employees on the estate.

At present the other five factories on the estate, making up two-thirds of the factory floor space, are vacant. One firm in particular illustrates the problems of the area: Maydown Precision Engineering is a co-operative formed by the workers of Molins Ltd which closed here in October 1984. Many of the skilled men they had employed were offered jobs in Molins' other factory in Peterborough; not many accepted the offer. The majority of them decided to fight to save the factory. They agreed to a 17½% wage cut and negotiated a contract with Molins for the sale of the co-operative's products.

Frank Hanna, their new chairman, says that a big plus point for the new company is the dynamic drive of the workforce who are determined to succeed. But the future depends on finding new markets and new orders.

Fig. 7.17. The logo for LEDU.

LEDU

The Local Enterprise Development Unit (LEDU) was set up in 1971. Its purpose is to promote employment in small firms with fewer than 50 employees. The government has recently been putting more emphasis on encouraging this type of firm. There are three reasons for this change of strategy:

1. The number of large 'footloose' firms from abroad willing to invest in Northern Ireland has declined.
2. Experience has shown that small, local companies stay in business longer. During the economic recession, British companies like Molins Ltd are more inclined to close, withdrawing their subsidiary companies from the province.
3. LEDU jobs cost less to promote – only about £4,000 each on average. LEDU's activity, by March 1984, had promoted about 19,000 jobs, a hopeful sign for the future.

Exercises

1. The location of Herdman's Mill results in the firm paying high transport costs for both imported raw materials and exported yarn. Suggest reasons why the firm has kept production in Sion Mills despite these high transport costs.
2. Study the flow diagram of costs in industry (fig. 7.1). Which factors have been most important in the changing fortunes of shipbuilding at Harland and Wolff?
3. Write a report for the Minister of Economic Development outlining the Government's case for spending money on attracting new industry to Northern Ireland.
4. What advantages would you emphasise in order to persuade the owner of a precision engineering firm located in Kent to expand and open a branch in Northern Ireland?
5. Discuss the reasons why manufacturing industries have grown up around Belfast.

 Exchanging goods and services

Internal transport

'The Belfast stage coach goes no further than Carrickfergus. From there to the next village, Larne, a two-horse cart conveys the traveller, who on his arrival there, must himself provide his own conveyance, or join Her Majesty's letter-bag which is carried northwards by a one-horse car.'

This is how a traveller described the journey out of Belfast in 1844. By today's standards travel then was extremely slow, tedious and uncomfortable. The journey from Belfast to Londonderry, for example, took a little over thirteen hours and it took over five hours to get from Newry to Dungannon.

Travel was also much more expensive. The journey by mail coach from Belfast to Dublin would have cost about the same as a labourer's wages for a whole month (it was only half that price though for an *outside* seat!). As a result, travel by coach was a luxury well beyond the reach of many.

Yet even in these early days there was quite a lot of traffic between large towns. In the late 1830s Belfast was linked with other places by fifty-three regular services. The mail-coach service to Londonderry carried about 3,000 passengers per year and about the same number travelled by this service between Belfast and Enniskillen.

Railways

The first section of railway line in Northern Ireland was opened in 1839 between Belfast and Lisburn. The next thirty years was a period of tremendous expansion as a **network** of railway lines was built across the province (see fig. 8.1).

There were two parts of the country where railways were difficult to construct. One was the Antrim Plateau to the north of Belfast and the other was across the drumlin belt of South Armagh and County Down. The need for railway track to have a gentle **gradient** made the southern edge of the Antrim Plateau a difficult barrier to get over. Once on top of the plateau there were also many boggy areas where foundations for the track were difficult to secure. In the drumlin belt to the south of Belfast the problem was one of straightening the winding route between the drumlins. Roads were able to follow the natural route, but railways required much more gently curving bends. So a great deal of earth-moving had to be done cutting through drumlins to lay track through this area. Despite these problems, the railways pushed north and south, linking Belfast with Coleraine and Londonderry in the north, and with Dublin in the south by the early 1860s.

By about 1870 Northern Ireland's railway network had reached its maximum extent.

The effects of the railways were felt in at least three ways:

network
An arrangement of routes which join and cross one another at junctions.

railway gradient
The degree of slope on a section of track. The maximum gradient on normal track is 1:100.

Fig. 8.1. Northern Ireland's railway network: (a) 1920 (b) 1960 (c) 1985.

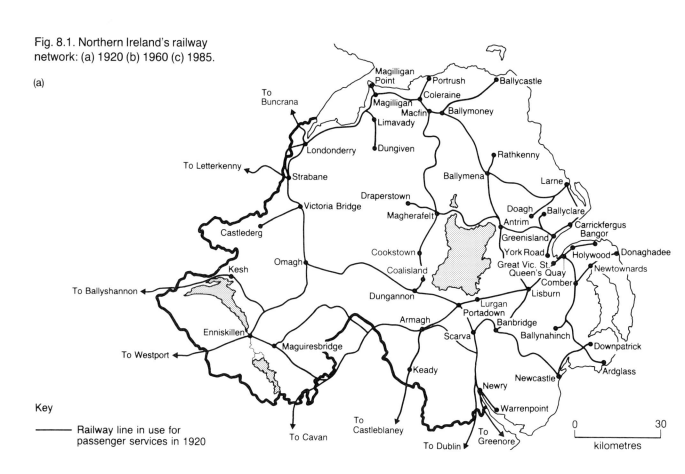

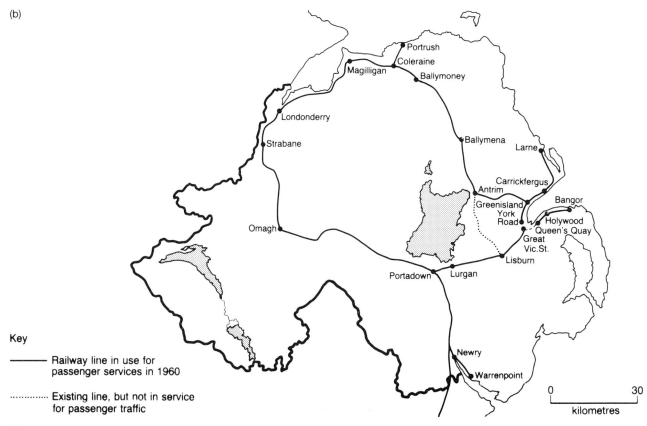

(c)

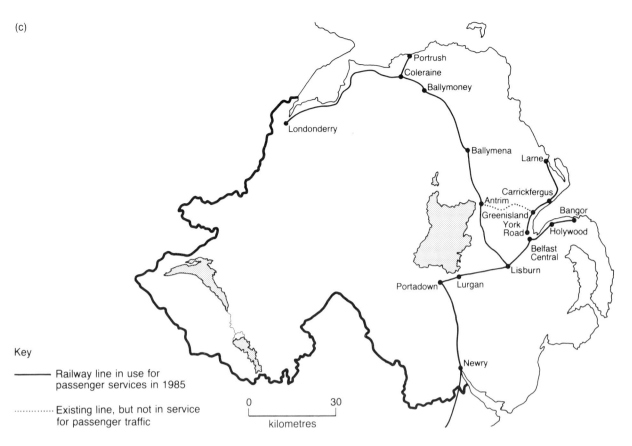

1. Travel time. In 1850 the mail coaches were travelling between Belfast and Dublin in about twelve hours. The railway was able to cover the same distance (about 150 km) in just over five hours.
2. Social conditions. The introduction of first-, second- and third-class carriages on trains helped to make travel less expensive. Ordinary working people could now afford to travel further than ever before. This was one of the factors which led to the expansion of holiday resorts like Bangor, Newcastle and Portrush.
3. Movement of freight. The railway made it possible for large amounts of heavy and bulky industrial goods to be moved quickly from one place to another. This helped to encourage the expansion of factory production.

In the 1920s the railways began to experience competition from road transport (see fig. 8.2). Few people could afford their own cars at first, but bus companies began carrying fare-paying passengers. Road haulage firms also began to compete for the transport of freight.

Road transport had a number of advantages over rail:

1. The political factor. Ireland was partitioned in 1922. This affected both the rail and road networks, but railway companies suffered more than road hauliers because they owned their own railway track. Some railway companies found their property divided between two states by the new border. This made it more difficult for them to operate efficiently. Road hauliers could simply adjust their routes to suit themselves.
2. The cost factor. As fig. 8.2 shows, the cost of transporting goods by road starts off low but rises sharply as the distance increases. The cost by rail is much higher for short distances but tapers off as distance

Fig. 8.2. The cost factor.

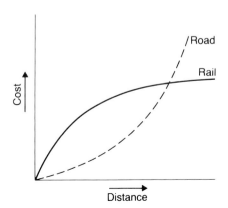

Fig. 8.3. The vicious circle of declining transport.

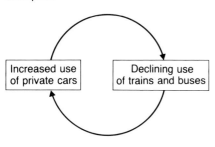

increases. So railways are best used for long routes. But Northern Ireland is so small it doesn't have any: the whole province is only 136 km long and 178 km wide.

3. The distribution of industry. Within this small province most industry is concentrated around Belfast and Londonderry. The result is that *most* freight traffic does not move outside a limited area – within 45 km of Belfast. This made it difficult for railways to compete with road transport for this business.
4. The flexibility of road traffic. Road traffic can go from door to door rather than from station to station. Routes between where you start and your destination can be changed. The times of travel are also easily adjusted to meet individual needs. There is also the comfort factor; with a private car there is no need to wait outdoors on cold or wet days.

(a) Can you add any advantages to this list?
(b) What are the advantages which rail transport *still* has over roads?

The result of this competition from roads was the closure of many railway lines in thinly populated areas (see fig. 8.1). Increasing numbers of private cars from 1950 onwards finally removed more than half the passenger traffic from the railways. A vicious circle of declining public transport had set in (fig. 8.3).

The number of vehicles on the roads increased from 79,000 in 1949 to 342,000 in 1969. During the same period the length of railway over which services were provided fell from 1,358 km to 323 km.

Today Northern Ireland Railways survives by concentrating on passenger services on a limited number of routes. Commuter services run from Belfast to Craigavon, Bangor and Larne. Long-distance services operate to Londonderry, Portrush and Dublin. A new central station opened in Belfast in 1976 (fig. 8.4). This linked the Bangor and Dublin lines. It is also planned to link the Larne line with Central Station via a new bridge across the River Lagan.

Fig. 8.4. Central Station, Belfast.

Fig. 8.5. A section of the West Link dual carriageway connecting the M1 and M2 in Belfast.

Roads

Government policy since the 1950s has favoured roads rather than railways. The Roads Act of 1948 introduced the plan for a trunk road network in Northern Ireland. Since then the Department of the Environment (the government department responsible for roads) has been involved in a massive road building and improvement scheme. At present there are 640 km of trunk roads and 111 km of motorway (figs. 1.1 and 8.5). The M1 motorway runs from Belfast to Dungannon (64 km) while the M2 runs from the docks area in Belfast north towards Londonderry. The trunk road network has been constructed to link these motorways with Armagh, Enniskillen, Omagh, Strabane, Londonderry and Coleraine and to provide by-passes around centres such as Dungannon, Ballymoney, Ballymena and Holywood. The main route south to Newry and Dublin has also been improved: it now by-passes Hillsborough, Dromore and Banbridge. These towns had all been previously congested by through traffic.

All of these improvements to the road network are designed to help people and goods move efficiently around the country. One way of trying to predict this movement is to use a gravity flow model (fig. 8.6).

Fig. 8.6. A gravity flow model.

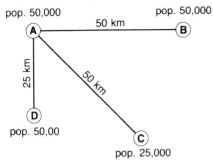

Study fig. 8.6 and decide which two towns you think would have most traffic passing between them.

You might expect more traffic between A and B than between A and C. The distances are the same but C has fewer people than B. Towns D and B are equally large but since D is closer to A there would probably be more traffic on this route than on the one between A and B.

The relationship between size of settlements, their distance apart and the flow of traffic between them is the basis of the gravity model. It can be expressed in a simple formula:

$$\text{Relative value of E} = \frac{\text{Population town A} \times \text{Population town B}}{\text{Distance between A and B}}$$

Table 13 *Factors affecting the gravity flow model in Northern Ireland.*

Distance (km)

	Armagh	Dungannon	Portadown	Lurgan	Banbridge	Newry
Armagh						
Dungannon	23					
Portadown	19	32				
Lurgan	30	39	11			
Banbridge	37	61	19	11		
Newry	35	60	35	35	25	
Newcastle	72	96	54	25	35	56

Population

Town	1981 census population
Armagh	12,700
Dungannon	8,295
Portadown	21,333
Lurgan	20,991
Banbridge	9,650
Newry	19,426
Newcastle	6,246

Example: Armagh – Dungannon

$$\text{Relative value of E} = \frac{12{,}700 \times 8{,}295}{23 \text{ km}} = 4.580$$

This formula has been used to calculate the expected traffic flow (E) values between towns in the southern part of the province (see fig. 8.7).

Using the information in Table 13, complete fig. 8.7 by calculating the expected flow values for traffic between Newry and Armagh, Portadown and Banbridge.

The actual traffic flows recorded on these roads in August 1982 are shown on fig. 8.8.

Plot the expected (E) values and the actual traffic flows on a **scattergraph** to examine the relationship between them. Answer the following questions:
(a) Is there a close relationship between the two sets of data?
(b) Are there any traffic flows which were not accurately predicted? If so, which ones?
(c) With the help of an atlas map of Northern Ireland and maps in this book, attempt to explain the pattern of traffic flow in fig. 8.8.
(d) Can you think of any factors which the gravity flow model fails to take into account?

Fig. 8.7. Predicted and actual flows of traffic between towns in the southern part of the province in August 1982.

	Values of E	Actual flow
1 Armagh–Dungannon	4.580	4,500
2 Armagh–Newry		3,750
3 Armagh–Portadown	14.259	8,000
4 Portadown–Dungannon	5.530	6,000
5 Portadown–Lurgan	40.709	12,000
6 Portadown–Newry		2,800
7 Lurgan–Banbridge	18.415	5,800
8 Banbridge–Newry		7,500
9 Banbridge–Newcastle	1.722	2,000
10 Newry–Newcastle	2.166	2,200

scattergraph
A graph which shows any trend in the relationship between two factors by the pattern of points on the graph.

External communications

Ports

The province's location on the edge of Europe, its lack of resources and

Fig. 8.8. Traffic flow, 1982.

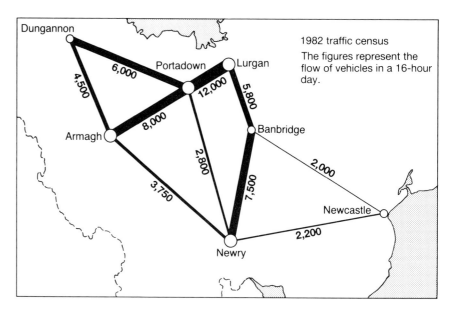

its small population make it very dependent on external communications. Northern Ireland has five commercial ports: Belfast, Larne, Warrenpoint, Londonderry and Coleraine. Their locations are shown on fig. 8.9. Some of these ports are much busier than others, depending on whether or not they have
(a) a sheltered location with deep water;
(b) space for the storage of freight;
(c) an industrial and densely populated hinterland;
(d) good transport links with that hinterland; and
(e) short sea links with other ports.

As far as shelter is concerned, only the north coast is unprotected from Atlantic storms. Two of the five commercial ports are located here but both of them are protected from the open sea. Coleraine is tucked away behind a sand bar, 7 kilometres from the mouth of the River Bann. Londonderry is protected because it is at the head of a large sea inlet. Belfast and Warrenpoint harbours are sheltered in the same way on the east coast. Larne harbour is probably the most exposed of the five, but it gets some protection hiding behind Islandmagee.

Looking at a map of Northern Ireland's coastline, Strangford Lough would seem to be a very good location for a port – yet it is the only large inlet from the coast without one. The main reason for this is that Strangford Lough is too shallow. Even some of the existing ports have had problems with their deep-water access. In chapter 7 you read how Belfast's industrial growth in the nineteenth century was hindered by its shallow harbour. Since then things have obviously improved. Today the port of Belfast has a straight channel 10 metres deep extending 10 kilometres out into the lough.

Coleraine harbour is troubled by silting in the River Bann and sand accumulation at the bar mouth. Costly dredging helps to maintain access to the port by a navigation channel 4 metres deep (minimum). Even Warrenpoint harbour, opened in 1974, has not been able to get its **roll-on/roll-off service** operating because improvements are needed to navigation in Carlingford Lough.

Space for storage can be another limiting factor. Belfast, by far the biggest port in the province, also has the most space for storage and

roll-on/roll-off service
Facilities which permit vehicles to drive, rather than be hoisted, on and off a ship.

Fig. 8.9. The commercial ports of Northern Ireland.

container trade
The use of standard-sized steel boxes for transporting freight by ship. These can be easily carried on a lorry. One container usually forms the complete load for one lorry.

expansion. Extensive land reclamation has created over 60 hectares for development. Warrenpoint has the advantage of a purpose-built site with 11 hectares of back-up area. Room for storage and expansion is more limited at the other ports.

The existence of a good hinterland is a crucial factor for a port's development. Belfast and Larne have a clear advantage over the other ports in this respect. Population and industry are concentrated in the east. The road and rail networks also focus on these ports. Larne competes with Belfast's hinterland for trade. Though Larne is much smaller it has prospered by concentrating on the roll-on/roll-off **container trade** and passenger transport (fig. 8.10). It has the advantage of the shortest and cheapest sea crossing to Britain. Between them, Sealink and Townsend-Thoresen are able to operate up to thirty-two arrivals and departures per day. Pandoro Ltd provides freight services to Fleetwood and Liverpool. Belfast harbour has concentrated on the import and export of traditional bulk cargoes, although Belfast Car Ferries does operate a nightly ferry service to Liverpool.

The province's other commercial ports have poorer hinterlands. Londonderry is a sizeable commercial and industrial area but, like Warrenpoint, it has to rely on attracting some trade from across the border with the Republic of Ireland. Coleraine is a small market town in a mainly agricultural area. Its main imports are coal and timber and its main exports are potatoes and other agricultural produce.

Airports

Belfast International Airport is situated at Aldergrove, about 23 kilometres north-west of the city. Nearly 1½ million passengers and approximately 16,000 tonnes of freight and mail pass through it each year. This makes it the seventh busiest airport in the United Kingdom. Regular services operate to sixteen cities in Britain by British Airways

Fig. 8.10. The roll-on, roll-off facilities at Larne.

Fig. 8.11. A British Airways Boeing 757 aircraft preparing for take-off at Belfast International Airport.

Table 14 *Passenger traffic from Belfast International Airport.*

Area of origin	Proportion of passengers (% of total)
Belfast	38
County Antrim	18
County Londonderry	8
County Tyrone	6
County Fermanagh	1
County Armagh	8
County Down	18
Republic of Ireland	5

and British Midland Airways (fig. 8.11).

The flight to London takes just over an hour. In the summer there are also direct flights from Belfast to many European resorts, and charter flights operate to the United States and Canada.

The airport's facilities have been improved enormously since the 1970s. A £23-million scheme has involved:
(a) doubling the size of the terminal buildings;
(b) constructing a new pier for domestic and international passengers;
(c) extending the main runway to 2,774 metres so that it can receive jumbo jets;
(d) installing new navigational equipment and ground lighting;
(e) building new car parks and changing the road system.

It's not just an airport's facilities that help to make it a success, though: access to and from an airport is also an important factor. You can judge how accessible Aldergrove is to the rest of the country by looking at figs. 1.1 and 8.1. Table 14 shows the proportion of outgoing passengers coming from various areas.

1. Are these the proportions you would have expected?
2. Do any of the figures surprise you?
3. Can you see any pattern to the figures? If so, what factors might be helping to produce this pattern? (You may find the population map on p. 13 helpful.)

An airport which is situated close to a large centre of population has the advantage of being able to attract passengers easily. It can also have the disadvantage of disturbing lots of people with aircraft noise! Fortunately this is not a serious problem at Aldergrove. Flight paths are able to follow a route over Belfast Lough, and the 23 kilometres between the coast and the airport is a rural farming area with a low-density population living mostly in single farmhouses.

The noise hazard is much more of a problem for the province's second airport, Belfast Harbour Airport, although it has some physical advantages (see Table 15).

This airport is operated by the aircraft firm, Short Brothers and Harland. It has one 2,000-metre runway and radar. Its terminal and passenger handling facilities are basic but efficient (fig. 8.12). While the Harbour Airport does not have the sophisticated facilities of Belfast International, it does have two big advantages:
1. It is less than ten minutes' drive from the centre of Belfast and within easy reach of motorways.
2. It is much cheaper for airlines to use because its overheads are low.

Three airlines – Loganair, Spacegrand and Manx Airlines – operate scheduled services from the Harbour Airport. Between them they fly to Glasgow, Edinburgh, the Isle of Man, Blackpool, Manchester, Liverpool and Teeside.

Expansion at this airport is limited by the following:
1. Technical difficulties. Since there is only one runway, landing and take-off are difficult in cross winds. There are also a number of potential hazards near the flight path: hills on each side of the Lagan Valley in which Belfast is situated, the giant cranes of Harland and Wolff shipyard and the large population of the city.
2. The noise factor. A night curfew operates and jets are not allowed for scheduled services from this airport, because it is in an urban area. In 1983 it was thought that DC9 jets might be permitted. Local reaction was mixed. The Lord Mayor at the time, Councillor Tommy Patton, said, 'People have taken out big mortgages for their homes. Young

Table 15 *Physical factors affecting Belfast's airports.*

	1941–70		
	Days with fog	Days with gales	Altitude
Belfast International	12	3.4	68 m
Belfast Harbour	7	10.0	3 m

Fig. 8.12. Passengers boarding a Shorts 363 aircraft at Belfast Harbour Airport.

people will be disturbed at night, falling asleep at their desks the next day and their education suffering.' Mr Wesley Pentland, a local Assembly member, said that the noise was greatly exaggerated. People should be glad of the jobs any expansion of the airport would bring.

3. The Civil Aviation Authority. This is the organisation which licences air routes. So far it has not allowed airlines to expand services from the Harbour Airport. The main reason seems to be a fear of what might happen to services operated from its competitor at Aldergrove.

What do *you* think would happen?

Exercises

1. Declining public transport has a particularly serious effect on rural communities. Suggest which groups of people living in rural areas suffer most.
2. The extent to which a network gives easy access or otherwise to places linked in it can be measured in the following way:
   (a) Count the number of links which exist in the network
   (b) Calculate the maximum number of *possible* links for a network with this number of nodes. This can be calculated using the formula:
   No. of possible links = 3 × (No. of nodes − 2)
   (c) Calculate the efficiency of the network as a percentage thus:

   $$\frac{\text{Actual links}}{\text{Possible links}} \times 100 = \text{Efficiency of network}$$

   There were 62 links in Northern Ireland's railway network in 1920, connecting 53 nodes. Its efficiency is calculated as:

   $$\frac{62}{3(53-2)} \times 100 = 40.5\%$$

   Calculate the efficiency of the network in 1960 and in 1985. (Remember, the higher the percentage figure, the more efficient the network is in giving access to the places linked in it.)

   This method does not take into account places left unconnected at the two later dates as the network declined.

   Calculate and compare the efficiency of the network in 1960 and 1985 once again, this time inserting the 53 nodes which existed in 1920 into the formula.
3. Write a report for the Minister of Transport justifying his policy of spending more money on roads than on railways in Northern Ireland.
4. Why is it useful to be able to predict the volume of traffic between places in a network?
5. Compare Belfast International and Belfast Harbour airports by giving each a score between 0 and 3 for each of the following factors:
   Flat land
   Room for expansion
   Airport terminal facilities
   Within easy travel distance of a large population
   Few people living near flight paths
   Automatic landing possible in poor weather
   No obstructions in flight path
   Low operating costs.
   What do you consider are the three main advantages that Belfast International Airport has over Belfast Harbour Airport for future development?
6. Conduct a class enquiry into the possibility of scheduled jet services operating from Belfast Harbour Airport next year. Elect a chairperson and allocate roles to groups representing various interested parties.

9 Northern Ireland in context

The people

In the context of the United Kingdom, Northern Ireland has a smaller population than Wales, Scotland or any English region. Yet the people of this small province have gained a reputation out of all proportion to their numbers: a reputation for both good and bad. Northern Irish people have become well known for both their sense of humour and their intolerance, for generosity and an inability to compromise. They are known for their friendliness towards strangers and their strong distrust of each other. These characteristics arise from the deep sectarian divisions in the community.

The civil strife resulting from these divisions has had many effects. As we saw in chapter 6, it has produced segregated residential areas in most parts of the province, particularly in west Belfast. It also affects political decision-making and provokes arguments about the distribution of government resources. The effect of the 'troubles' on tourism can be seen in fig. 9.1. While the number of visitors to the Irish Republic increased by 17% between 1968 and 1982, the number of visitors to the North during the same period dropped by 45%. The largest decrease was one of 53% in the number of British tourists visiting Northern Ireland. But the most significant figure was a fourfold increase in the number of tourists from outside Europe (mainly Americans) visiting the Republic. This is perhaps an indication of what might have been had the 'troubles' not put off many potential holidaymakers from visiting the North.

Fig. 9.1. Visitors to Northern Ireland and the Republic of Ireland, 1968 and 1982.

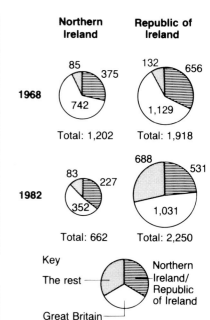

Origin of visitors staying more than one day	To Northern Ireland (thousands)		% change	To Republic of Ireland (thousands)		% change
	1968	1982	1968–82	1968	1982	1968–82
Northern Ireland	—	—	—	656	531	−19
Republic of Ireland	375	227	−40	—	—	—
Great Britain	742	352	−53	1,129	1,031	−9
Rest of the world	85	83	−2	132	688	+421
Total	1,202	662	−45	1,918	2,250	+17

| Day visitors | 8,350 | 4,000 | −52 | 15,356 | 7,544 | −51 |

The economy

As we saw in chapter 7, civil unrest has also had an effect on the economy of Northern Ireland. It is ironic that while the 'troubles' have reduced the will to invest, they have also stimulated the natural growth of jobs in the public service sector! One economist's evaluation of the effects of the 'troubles' on employment is shown in Table 16. While bombings and shootings make headlines and have some effect, they are not the main cause of the province's economic difficulties. Even without civil unrest it is likely that Northern Ireland would still be economically weak in comparison with other parts of the United Kingdom and Europe. This is because her position on the edge of Europe seriously hinders industrial expansion. Northern Ireland suffers from the problems of a peripheral region: a small home market, high transport costs, few resources and the problem of keeping in touch with new ideas. In contrast, as fig. 9.2 shows, north-west Europe is a core area: it has become established as a centre for many industries. These industries act like a magnet for other industries attracted to the region by the advantages of agglomeration.

Table 16 *Effect of the 'troubles' on employment in Northern Ireland, 1970–80, according to one economist.*

	Change	% of 1970
Agriculture	nil	nil
Manufacturing	−25,000	−14
Other industry	−4,000	−4.5
Private services	−10,000	−8
Public services	+15,000	+14
Total	−24,000	−4

In October 1984, nearly 120,000 people were out of work in Northern Ireland. The overall unemployment rate was 20.4% compared with 14.2% for the United Kingdom as a whole. This was by far the highest regional unemployment rate. In 1981/82 average weekly income per household in Northern Ireland was £134.10, and spending averaged £116.20. Almost 11% of this went on fuel, light and power. This was nearly double the average for England. The proportion spent on food, tobacco, clothing and footwear were also higher than elsewhere. In contrast, households in the province spent lower proportions of their income on housing, alcohol and durable goods than those in any other region of the United Kingdom. Proportionately fewer households in Northern Ireland possess central heating, a washing machine, a fridge, a television and a telephone. This confirms the province's position as the poorest of the eleven regions in the United Kingdom.

In an Irish context, Northern Ireland makes up 20% of the island's land area with 45% of its population. When the border was introduced in 1921 it separated a predominantly agricultural South from the more industrialised North. In chapter 1 we saw that once borders become established, differences between the two sides develop over the years. One of the major differences to appear has been in the attitudes of the governments of the United Kingdom and the Republic of Ireland towards borrowing money for industrial expansion. In the 1970s, government in the Republic was much more willing to do this. As a member of the European Monetary System (EMS) – which the United Kingdom declines to join – it also became cheaper for the Republic to borrow. This resulted in higher investment in new industry there than in the North. The amount of financial help to industry in the two parts of Ireland during the period 1975–81 is shown in Table 17. Grants and loans obtained from the EEC for Southern industry were four times greater than those going to the North.

During the same period, all UK government aid to Northern Ireland industry amounted to **ECU** 830 million and the Republic's grants to industry were ECU 1,300 million.

ECU
European Community Unit, a standard monetary unit for EEC finances.

Table 17 *EEC investment assistance to industry in Northern Ireland and the Republic of Ireland, 1975–81 (ECU million).*

		Northern Ireland	Republic of Ireland
EEC investment	Grants	372	732
	Loans	198	1,288
Government investment	Grants	830	1,300
Total		1,390	3,310

In a period when Northern Ireland's traditional industries were in decline, the Republic's high levels of investment proved quite successful in generating jobs. As a result the economies and the standards of living in the two parts of Ireland have grown more alike.

Table 18 shows some social and economic indicators. It shows that the Republic now earns a higher proportion of its total GDP from industry than Northern Ireland does.

1. How do hourly earnings in industry compare?
2. What do the figures reveal about the general standard of living in Northern Ireland compared with the Republic?
3. How does the standard of living in Ireland, North and South, compare with Great Britain?

Differences in standard of living are one reason why Ireland, North and South, has traditionally exported one of its most valuable commodities: people. The Irish habit of moving away has drained both economies of their most talented, young, enthusiastic 'go-getters'. In the 1970s Northern Ireland lost at least one-tenth of its population. Most of this flow went to Britain. With a birth rate of over 17 per 1,000, the proportion of young people in Northern Ireland is increasing. Can this growing resource be used? As the slogan for the Industrial Development Authority in the Republic declares, 'People are to Ireland as oil is to Texas'. This growing young population can either add to the present problem of unemployment or be used as part of the solution.

Fig. 9.2. The EEC: core and periphery.

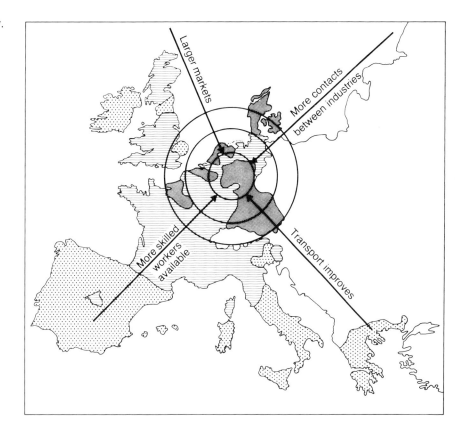

Key

GDP per head, 1977

More than $8,000

$4,000–$8,000

Less than $4,000

Table 18 *Social and economic indicators.*

	Northern Ireland	Republic of Ireland	Great Britain
% of total GDP (1980)			
in agriculture	6	11	7
industry	30	33	34
services	64	56	59
Average hourly earnings in industry (1981) IR£	3.20	3.36	3.61
Personal disposable income (1981) IR£	2,529	2,444	3,107
Cars per 1,000 people (1981)	233	210	277
Telephones per 1,000 people (1982)	246	224	515

Answers to questions on p. 17.
2. (a) Londonderry and Newry and Mourne.
   (b) Only in Belfast and its neighbouring districts, in Craigavon and in Fermanagh are more than 5% of the population Methodists.
   (c) In almost all denominations about 48% are male.

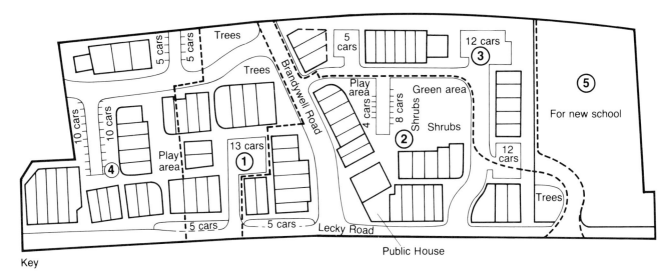

Key

[1] Boundary of area of phased redevelopment

A professional plan for the redevelopment of the Brandywell area, Londonderry.

Index

Page numbers in italics refer to tables or illustrations.

Abercorn, 70
affluence, 18, *19*
airports, *4*, 87–9
Aldergrove, 87–9
amenity index, 66
Antrim, 21, 27, 55, 81
    population, 12, 14, 15, *45*
Armagh, 22, 45, 46, 81, 84
Armoy moraine, 23

Ballintoy, 28
Ballycastle, 26, 27
Ballymena, *45*, 78, 84
Ballymagroarty, *49*
Ballymoney, 84
Banbridge, 84
Bangor, 14, 44, 47–8, 65, 83, 84
Bann (River/Valley), 22, 23, 27, *37*, 38
bauxite, 27
Belfast, 38, 44, 47, 54–63
    airport, 87–9
    housing, 58–9
    population, *13*, 14–15
    port, 86–7
    transport, 56–8, 60, 81, 84, 86–9
Belfast Car Ferries, 87
Belfast Harbour Airport, 88–9
Belfast International Airport, 87–8
Belfast Telegraph, 63
Belgium, 70
Bessbrook, 51
Binevenagh, 21
birth rate, 73, 92
Black Mountain, 27
Boeing 757 (aircraft), *88*
boundaries, 5–10
Brandywell, 53, *94*
British Airways, 87, 88
British Isles, 5
British Midland Airways, 87–8
Brownlow (Craigavon), 64
Burn Dennet, 28
Burngibbagh, 28
Bush (River), 29
Bushmills, 13

Caledon, 51
Caledonian Mountains, 21
Camlough Pump Storage scheme, 38
capital, 67
car ownership, 56, *57*, 60
Carlingford Lough, 6, 23, 86
Carrickfergus, 14, 46, 46, 47
Castle Archdale, 25, 40, *41*
Castlereagh, 14, *61*
Castlewellan, 46
cattle, 30–1, 34
Cavan, 7, 26
cavity wall insulation, 17, *18*
CBD (Central Business District), 55–6
census, 11–19
Central Station (Belfast), 84

chalk, 27, 28
Charlemont, 46
chickens, 34
Civil Aviation Authority, 89
clachan, 45
clay, 27, 28
climate, 24–5, 29, *31*, *89*
Cloghmore Rock, 22, *24*
Clonard, 61–3
coal, 26
Coalisland, 26, 27, 28
Coleraine, 46, 81, 84, 86, 87
Conlig, *17*, 48
containers, 87
Cookstown, 12
core, *93*
correlation, 19
corries, 22
counterurbanisation, 15
Craigavon, 12, 14, 63–5, *66*, 84
Creggan, *49*
Cromac Redevelopment Area, 60
Crumlin, 28
Cushendun, *52*

dairy farming, 32, *33*
Dalriada, 5
DC9 (aircraft), 88
demand, 73
Derry, *see* Londonderry
'Direct Rule', 76
Donaghadee, 47
Donegal, 7, 28
dot distribution map, 14
Down, 21, 22, 55, 81
    population, 14, 15, *45*, 47, *48*
Downpatrick, 45
Draperstown, *46*
drift, 23
Dromore, 84
drumlins, 22–3, *24*
Dublin, 81, 83, 84
Dungannon, 46, 81, 84

ecosystem, 30
ECU (European Currency Unit), 92
EEC (European Economic Community), 9, 32, 92, *93*
Eglinton, 51
electricity, 74–5
    see also HEP
employment, 73–9, 91
EMS (European Monetary System), 92
energy sources, 27–8, 29, *37*, 38, 74–5
    see also fuels; HEP; water; as source of power
England, 5
English Channel, 5
Enniskillen, 46, 81, 84
Erne (Lough), 12, 25
erratics, 22, *24*
eskers, 23

'factory' farming, 33–5
Fairhead, 13
famine, 15, 49, 51
farming, 30–5, *42*
fashion, 69
Faughan (River), 28
Fermanagh, 12, 22, *23*, 26, 28
forecasting, 15–16
forests, forestry, 25, 36–7
Foyle (River), 5–6, 28
    Bridge, *48*, 49, 73
France, 5
fuels, *27*

gentrification, 47
geology, 21–9
Giant's Causeway, 13, 21
glaciation, 22–4
Glasgow Celtic FC, 63
Glenshesk Valley, 25
Glenwhirry water scheme, 37–8
'Goliath', 72, 88
Gracehill, 51
gradient, 81
gravity flow model, 84–5
Great Britain, 5, 7
Groomsport, 47

Hanna, Frank, 80
Harland, Edward, 71
Harland and Wolff, 71–3, 88
HEP (Hydroelectric power), *37*, 38
Herdman Mill, 70–1
hierarchy, 44, 45
Hilden Mill, 47
Hillsborough, 46, 84
hinterland, 87
Hivolt Capacitors Ltd, 79
Holywood, 47, 48
housing, 48–50, 51–2
    in Belfast, 58–61
    in Craigavon, 64

igneous rocks, 21
Industrial Development Authority (Irish Republic), 92
industry, 67–80, 92
    decline in, 73–4
    government aid to, 74–9
    linen, 67–71
    shipbuilding, 71–3
inheritance, 51
IRA (Irish Republican Army), 75
Irish Commission (1925), *8*
Irish News, 63
Irish Republic, 5–9, 90–3
Irish Sea, 5
Island Reavy (Lough), 37
Italy, 71

Joy Street (Belfast), 60, *61*
jumbo jet (Boeing 747), 88

Keady, 30
Kells, 37
Kilkeel-Cranfield moraine, 23
Kilroot, 28
Kinnahalla water scheme, *36*, 37–8
Knocklayd, 13

Lagan (Valley/River), 21, 39, 55, 84, 88
Lambeg Industrial Research Institute, 69
land use, 30–43, 55–6
   in CBD, 55–6
   farming, 30–5
   forestry, 36–7
   leisure, 39–42
   water supply, 37–8
Larne, 14, 26, 84, 86, 87, *88*
Larry Bane Head, 28
LEDU (Local Enterprise Development Unit), 79
leisure, *35*, 37, 39–42
Leitrim Hills, 6
Lifford, 5
lignite, 28, 29
Limavady, 46
limestone, 27
linen, 67–71
Lisburn, 14, 44, 81
Loganair, 88
Londonderry, *45*, 48–50, *52*
   transport, 81, 84, 86, 87
Long Bridge, 55
Lurgan, 44, 64

Magho Scarp, 21
Magilligan, 26
magma, 21
Mandeville (Craigavon), 64
manufacturing industry, 73–4
Manx Airlines, 88
Marble Arch, 21
Matthew, Sir Robert, 63
Maydown Industrial Estate, 79
Maydown Precision Eng. Ltd, 79
Michelin, 78–9
Midland Valley (Scotland), 21
migration, 14–16, 92
mixed farming, 30–2
Molins Ltd, 79
Monaghan, 7
moraine, 23
Mountjoy, 46
Mourne (River), *37*, 70
Mourne Mountains, 6, 21, 22
Moville, 5–6
Moyle, 13
Moyraverty centre (Craigavon), 64
Mulholland, Thomas and Andrew, 68
mushrooms, 33–4

Nash, John, 51
National Supply Co. (UK) Ltd, 79
Neagh (Lough), 21, 23, 25, 37
net output, 69
network, 81, 89

New Towns, 63
New World, 15
Newcastle, 83
Newry, 46, 81, 84
Newtownabbey, 14, 44
Newtownards, 14, 65
noise, 88–9
Normandy, 70
Northern Ireland Railways, 84
nunataks, 22

Oceanic, 71
oil, 72, 73
Omagh, 50, 84

Pandoro Ltd, 87
partition, 83
Patton, Tommy, 88–9
'peace line', *61*, *62*
peat, 25, *26*
Pentland, Wesley, 89
people, *see* population
periphery, *93*
Peter England Ltd, 79
Pettigoe, 6, *7*
pigs, 32, *33*, 34
planning, 48–50, 51–3
plates, 21
podzolic soils, 25, *26*
polder, *39*
Poleglass estate (Belfast), 61
politics, 76–9, 90
population, 11–19, 92
Portadown, 44, 46, 64
Portrush, 46, 83, 84
ports, 85–7
potatoes, 33
Pot of Legawherry, 22
Pot of Pulgarve, 22
power, *see* energy sources; fuels; HEP; water: as source of power
Poyntz Pass, 23
Pulgarve, 22

Radburn planning, 47
railways, 81–3
reclamation, 38, 87
recreation, *see* leisure
religion, 17, *18*, 76, *78*
   in Belfast, 61–3
residential segregation, 61–3
ribbon development, 47
roads, 38, 83–5, *86*
   in Belfast, 56–8
rocks, 21, 26–9
Roe (River), *39*
roll-on/roll-off service, 86, 87, *88*
Rostrevor, 22, *24*
rural settlement, 51–2

Sally-En, 5–6
salt, 27
'Samson', 72, 88
sandstone, 27

scattergraph, 85
Scotland, 5
sea wrack, 47
Sealink, 87
sectors, 74
sedimentary rocks, 21
services, 51
settlements, 44–52
Shankill, 61–3
shipbuilding, 71–3
Short Brothers and Harland, 88
Shorts 363 (aircraft), *89*
Sion Mills, 70, *71*
Slieve Binnian, 22
Slieve Commedagh, 22
Slieve Donard, 29
Slieve Gallion, 22
Slieve Muckish, *21*
Snare and Clayton Ltd, 79
social information, 17–19
soils, 25, *26*
Spacegrand, 88
Spearman's Rank Correlation, 19
Sperrin Mountains, 6, 22
Strabane, 5, 46, 84
Strangford Lough, *24*, *38*, 86
suburbs, 59, 61
Suffolk, *17*
supply, 73
SWOPS (Single Well Oil Production System), 73

television, 63
terminal moraine, 23
Termon (River), *7*
Titanic, 71
tourism, 39, *42*, 90
towns, 44–50
Townsend-Thoresen, 87
traffic, 56–7
transport, 56–9, 68, 74, 81–9
'troubles', 38, 57, 61–3, 75, 90–1
Tunny Point water scheme, 37–8

Ulster, 7, 15
Ulster Way, 40
unemployment, 76, *77*, 91
United Kingdom, 5, 6, 90–3
Upper Malone, 61
uranium, 28
urban field, 44–5
urban settlement, 44–50

vegetation, 25
villages, 51

Wales, 5
Warrenpoint, 9, 46, 86, 87
water, *36*, 37–8, 51
   as source of power, 55, 68, 70
West Link (Belfast), *84*
Windsor House, *55*
Wolff, Gustav, 71